Great to see you.
Bob Ban

"all the sincerity in hollywood . . ."

SELECTIONS *from the* WRITINGS
of RADIO'S LEGENDARY COMEDIAN

fred allen

TO ED & ANN
Best wishes—

Stuart Hample

"all the sincerity in hollywood . . ."

SELECTIONS *from the* WRITINGS
of RADIO'S LEGENDARY COMEDIAN

fred allen

*Compiled and with an Introduction
by Stuart Hample*

FULCRUM PUBLISHING

Golden, Colorado

Library of Congress Cataloging-in-Publication Data
Allen, Fred, 1894–1956.
All the sincerity in Hollywood— : selections from the writings of radio's
legendary comedian Fred Allen ? compiled and with an introduction
by Stuart Hample.
        p.   cm.
ISBN 1-55591-154-4 (hardcover)
1. Allen, Fred, 1894–1956—Correspondence.   2. Allen, Fred, 1894–1956—
Quotations.   3. American wit and humor.   I. Title: Selections from the writings
of radio's legendary comedian Fred Allen.   II. Hample, Suart E.   III. Title.
PN2287.A48 A38 2001
792.7'028'092—dc21
[B]
2001040223

Printed in the United States of America
0 9 8 7 6 5 4 3 2 1

Editorial: Marlene Blessing, Daniel Forrest-Bank, Alison Auch
Design: Trina Stahl
Cover image: Caricature of Fred Allen copyright © 1951 Al Hirschfeld. Drawing
reproduced by special arrangement with Hirschfeld's exclusive
representative, The Margo Feiden Galleries, New York.

Fulcrum Publishing
16100 Table Mountain Parkway, Suite 300
Golden, Colorado 80403
(800) 992-2908 • (303) 277-1623
www.fulcrum-books.com

To the memory of Lastone,
Portland's sister, Fred's late-night typist, Frances's mother,
who graciously gave her time, her memories, her friendship
and a wonderful lunch.

Who can confidently say what ignites a certain combination of words, causing them to explode in the mind.

—E. B. WHITE,
The Elements of Style

contents

acknowledgments

BECAUSE OF the following people's contributions, this project has turned out to be even more gratifying than one could have imagined.

Begin with Lastone Hoffa Hershkowitz (the Lastone from the dedication, so named because she was thought to be the last-born in her family), who in countless ways brought Fred Allen to vivid life and filled in many blanks. Her daughter, Frances, also generously shared memorabilia and personal recollections of her Aunt "Porty" and Uncle Fred (who, when repeatedly conscripted to be her babysitter, was discomfited because the kid interfered with his writing).

Mere words cannot begin to suggest the extent of the contributions made by the redoubtable Bob Baron, Fulcrum cofounder and publisher, second to no one in his affection for Fred Allen and his enthusiasm for this enterprise. Authors: know that Bob, in the tradition of the great publisher-proprietors of yore, has the courage and vision to issue a book based not on its bottom-line potential but on his passion for it.

Bernard Margolis, president of the Boston Public Library, who nurtured the project from the time it was merely a notion. Bobbie Zonghi and staff of the Rare Books and Manuscripts Department at the Boston Public Library, and especially Eugene Zepp, who followed every trail.

Allene White for permission to use the E. B. White excerpt, and for telling me, "E. B. was a great fan of Fred Allen's."

Tenor Robert White, who recalled details of his appearances on Allen's show and provided Fred's letter to his father about the Protestant cat. Norton Juster, for his editorial judgment and corrective verbal abuse. Geri Thoma, intrepid beyond belief, making The 400 seem like wimps by comparison. Dave Davis, for remembering his dad's witty (and accurate) comparison of radio and television. Stuart Canin, for his take on the Allen–Benny feud. Herman Wouk, for permission to include his perceptive letter to *The New York Times*. Vanessa Friedman, who took time from her busy London schedule to read early drafts of the proposal and offer sage advice. Amber Hiken, widow of the great Nat, for her recollections of Allen and the letters of his she provided. Wilfrid Sheed, who generously allowed me to quote from his W.C. Fields piece.

Al Hirschfeld, another hero of mine, who took time away from his drawing board and swung his famous barber chair round to speak about his longtime friend.

Will Grossman, the only medical doctor I know with no attitude, who patiently explained Allen's disease and its symptoms, confident that today's medicine could have helped him to live longer (and didn't send me a bill).

Joe LaRosa, for his unerring judgment. The fabulous Marlene Blessing, who cheerfully pulled it all together. Terry Steiner, for endless favors. Dan Forrest-Bank, who manned the trenches.

The late Kenny Delmar, aka Sen. Claghorn, who originally led me to Allen, and fed me in Hollywood when I was his stand-in for *It's A Joke, Son!*, in 1946 at Eagle–Lion Studio, next to Goldwyn Studio, on the same block with the Formosa Bar.

The late Noel Behn for leading me to Lastone.

The late Ed Herlihy for anecdotes about his sometime collaborator and first cousin.

The late Arnold Auerbach for inside stories from his experience as a young writer (partnered with Herman Wouk) on the Allen show.

A special tip of the hat to Herb Sargent, who is never late and always appears like magic to open another door when the trail turns cold.

Robert Taylor's *Fred Allen: His Life and Wit* (Little, Brown, 1989), a biography, and Alan Havig's *Fred Allen's Radio Comedy* (Temple University Press, 1990), a survey of Allen in the context of radio history and American humor, were a mother lode of inestimable help. These, along with Fred Allen's two memoirs, *Treadmill to Oblivion, Much Ado About Me,* and *Fred Allen's Letters,* comprise "The Five Books of Fred," the bible for Allen worshippers.

introduction

"For 17 years, amid a sea of mediocrity,
Fred Allen remained uncopied and unique."

—Newsweek

AMONG THE comedians of Radio's Golden Age, Fred Allen was the only one ever seriously called a satirist, the only one whose broad humor and knowing commentary appealed simultaneously to the man in the street and a cultlike following of intellectuals, the only one who ranks as a humorist. He was also one of the best-loved men of his time. Yet, except for cultural historians or old-time radio buffs, it's unlikely that anyone who is too young to remember when Dillinger was gunned down even knows his name.

A number of factors account for this lapse in our national collective memory. First, and perhaps most telling, Allen was the only one of his peers—Bob Hope, Jack Benny, George Burns, Jim Jordan (Fibber McGee), Edgar Bergen—whose career did not flourish also in television, a medium inimical to him. In radio, Allen was in total control of his shows. The script (which, because of his perfectionism and the constraints of censorship, became "drudgery" and eventually took a toll on his health) served as the foundation upon which everything else rested. At bottom Allen was a writer, a word man. There were no holes in his reason. His currency was the precise use of language—metaphors, rampant wordplay, rhymes, the unhurried turn of phrase, succinct aphorisms—rather than the situation-comedy formats, stock characters and standard joke forms employed by most other radio comedians. His bemused, shrewd commentaries upon the manners and morals of midcentury America were fueled by current events, which often do not travel well over time. You will presently discover, however, that various of his observations retain their bite. For instance, his disdain for Hollywood was legendary (see "allen v. hollywood," p. 78), and he pulled no punches, fearing neither studio heads nor powerful film colony columnists. Of a male celebrity who strode into church one midwinter morning wearing sunglasses, Allen said: "I guess he's afraid God might recognize him and ask for an autograph."

On his celebrated radio program in Depression and wartime America, Allen managed to lighten the spirits of 30 million demoralized, confused human beings weekly for seventeen years with words alone. In radio, where sound is everything, Fred Allen was at the top of his game.

But television is different; the script is merely another working part in the complex machinery. The TV performer is completely at the mercy of the packed production process. In this situation, the fiercely independent Allen (who was then suffering from critically high blood pressure) did not feel at home. Serving up his droll, penetrating humor in a hot, cable-strewn TV studio, bedeviled by a clutch of technical people, left him feeling gloomy and disgruntled. So much random activity swirling about stunned him, threw him off his rhythm, interfered with his sense of comedy. Too many people, too many voices. Allen, stubbornly idiosyncratic and methodical in the way he worked, did not suffer interference well. In his ill-fated TV turns, he appears to have lost confidence in his vaunted pace, timing and tone. Moving stiffly, he betrays a

certain wariness, devoid of the bravura of his great radio
stints. On one guest shot, he appears in drag, duped into cheap
slapstick. It's sad, rather like watching a former champion
whose gifts have diminished taking on one fight too many. His
appearances in movies, a form in which Hope, Burns and, to
some extent, Benny flourished, reflect the same discomfort
level and are mostly a disappointment. ("Photogenically I do
not come off too well," he conceded.) On radio he didn't need
to be seen to get laughs.

The upstart television, feeling its oats, didn't give a damn
that he had been the most endlessly inventive of the radio
comedians, or that before him, popular comedy did not
sting. The comedian whose image flickers each week on the
home screen is the comedian remembered. Fred Allen did not
flicker well.

He later wrote, presciently, "Whether he knows it or not
the comedian is on a treadmill to oblivion. When a radio comedian's program is finally finished it slinks down Memory Lane
into the limbo of yesterday's happy hours. All that the comedian has to show for his years of work and aggravation is the
echo of forgotten laughter."

Yet he may have had the last laugh. More than a half-
century after his radio show was consigned to the dustbin
of history, his effect on comedy endures. According to *American Heritage* magazine, "His influence on other comics, by
virtue of his remarkable generous assistance or direct example,
remains pervasive."

Fred Allen transformed popular comedy, giving our
Norman Rockwell country a kick in the britches by opening up
new areas for us to laugh at. He was the first in broadcasting to
lampoon news events, commercials, big business and puncti-
ious, puny-minded executives; the first to deconstruct popular

culture—including radio itself (the self-referential style of scores of contemporary shows, including *Late Night with David Letterman,* follows in his wake); the first to employ satire to deflate official humbug, pretension and the sacred. Allen took pot shots even at Old Man Death.

His 1930s show *Town Hall Tonight* was largely based upon news reports of life in a fictional small hamlet, a model for Lake Woebegone, the nexus of Garrison Keillor's *Prairie Home Companion.* Steve Allen's running characters—nervous Don Knotts, confused Tom Poston, lovably timid José Jimeinez, suave, smug adman Gordon Hathaway—are reminiscent of the denizens of "Allen's Alley," mainstays of the Allen Show in the 1940s (see page 14). Allen's early experiments with nonsense can safely be cited as having influenced Bob & Ray. He certainly affected the sensibility of *Saturday Night Live*—particularly the News Update segment (a direct descendant of a feature created by him), which was integral to the careers of Chevy Chase and Dennis Miller. *That Was The Week That Was,* created by David Frost for BBC, later adapted for American audiences by Herb Sargent, also fits the Allen mold of sending up topical subjects with irony, farce and satire. Allen had a never-fail instinct for how to exploit the potential laugh behind a news item and was, in effect, the radio cousin to the "Newsbreaks" (mostly written by E. B. White, an Allen hero), brief pieces that characterized the other new smartcracker kid in town in the thirties, *The New Yorker.* Johnny Carson concedes that his "Mighty Carson Art Players" was adapted from "The Mighty Allen Art Players." David Letterman acknowledges that he derived the notion for his off-beat interviews from Allen's feature "People You Didn't Expect to Meet."

The terminal irreverence of *Comedy Central,* the insolent observational style of topical comedians and talk show hosts, the iconoclastic humor of *Mad* and *National Lampoon,* as well as Sid Caesar's movie takeoffs on *Your Show of Shows* are arguably all Allen legatees.

Fred Allen was droll, rich in fantastic invention, a man of penetrating good humor and clear perception who limned life's absurdities with astringent wit. His barbs were wry, deliberate, a little sly, deftly flicked like acid-tipped shuttlecocks. He exuded singularity. No one, in any branch of show business, or even humanity, spoke in tones as flat-out funny as his God-granted nasal voice, a celebrated sound as distinctively Allen's as his DNA, variously described as "sounding like a man with false teeth chewing on slate pencils" . . . "like the dry crackle of brown wrapping paper" . . . "as if it might be filing his teeth down as it issues from his spigot mouth" . . . "a gravelly nasal rasp" . . . "with nutmeg-grater tones" . . . "a vinegar drawl" . . . "a parched, unhappy singsong" . . . and "purest sandpaper primordial wheeze." That voice was advantageous; as soon as he croaked out a word, people started to laugh.

Here's how his fellow writers rated him:

"Fred Allen is unquestionably the best humorist of our time. . . . A brilliant critic of manners and morals . . . who operates in the real medium of American humor in the manner of Petroleum Nasby, Eli Perkins, Mark Twain and their like."
—JOHN STEINBECK

"Fred Allen's hilarious, and sometimes chilling, seventeen years in radio may have been a treadmill for him, but it was a flight for me, more interesting than Lindbergh's. . . . You can count on the thumb of one hand the American who is at once a comedian, a humorist, a wit and a satirist, and his name is Fred Allen."
—JAMES THURBER

"He retained a fearless honesty and integrity . . . he hurled his wit in the face of sham wherever he saw it, raked fools and phonies with his barbed wit."

—IRVING WALLACE

"(His) saucy tomfoolery stole our hearts."

—S. J. PERELMAN

" . . . sharp of wit, gently acerbic, a keen observer of human foibles and the American scene."

—GOODMAN ACE

"Fred Allen is America's Voltaire, England's Ring Lardner . . . Spain's Heinrich Heine."

—GROUCHO MARX

" . . . a rare and wonderful man who, in spite of having written the finest comedy in the history of broadcasting, and in spite of having written literally hundreds of the wittiest and most felicitous letters of our time, did not for a moment consider himself to be a really good writer at all. I don't think Fred Allen was wrong in many things, but he was absolutely wrong in this."

—EDWIN O'CONNOR

And, when Allen died, Herman Wouk wrote to *The New York Times:*

The death of Fred Allen, America's greatest satiric wit in our time, brings to mind Hazlitt's elegiac paragraph on the Restoration actors:

'Authors after their deaths live in their works; players only in their epitaphs and the breath of common traditions. They die and leave the world no copy. . . . In a few years nothing is known of them but that they were.'

Fred Allen was an eminent comic actor. But without a doubt his great contribution to life in America came in the marvelous eighteen-year run of weekly satirical invention, which was *The Fred Allen Show* on radio. His was the glory of being an original personality, creating new forms of intelligent entertainment. He was without a peer and without a successful imitator.

His knife-like comment on the passing show of the thirties and the forties came from sources no other comedian had access to. He was a self-educated man of wide reading; he was a tremendously talented writer; and he had the deep reticent love of life and of people which is the source of every true satirist's energy. Fred's wit lashed and stung. He could not suffer fools. In this he was like Swift and like Twain. But his generosity to the needy, his extraordinary loyalty to his associates (in a field not noted for long loyalties) showed the warmth of heart that made his satire sound and important.

Because his work was a unique kind of comic journalism the written residue might have suffered the usual fate of journalism. Fred fortunately preserved a fraction of it in that fine volume of Americana . . . *Treadmill to Oblivion*. When he died, he was working on his autobiography (*Much Ado About Me*). . . .

But the few writings he left will give future generations a dim notion at best of what sort of man he was. In Fred Allen, the voice of sanity spoke out for all Americans to hear, during a trying period in our history, in the classic and penetrating tones of comic satire. Because he lived and wrote and acted here, this land will always be a saner place to live in. That fact is his true monument.

Allen ultimately found no fun in radio, the medium which gave him fame, wealth and security. "It is too much for me," he wrote near the beginning of his broadcast career. "I am all in. This is the nineteenth program, I think, and between routines for Portland [his wife and costar] and the rehearsals and cutting and editing the material . . . it finally begins to tell. . . . I have enough acid going on in me to turn all the gold wedding rings Mussolini took away from the married women of Italy black, and my nerves are going up and down like the heels of any welterweight you saw in 1921." In what was to be the final year of his weekly show, he was spent. "This is my seventeenth year of this drudgery. Unless we find some way of lightening the burden, I will have to look for something easier, like checking the altitude on tiddlywink chips for the American Aeronautical Old Age Group." Because of his nature, Fred Allen was foreordained to remain frustrated through the years—from FDR through Truman—he sent his meticulously crafted words out into the ether. Yet toil he did, acknowledged as the most intelligent comedian on the air.

Consider this: a rare outstanding comedy show on television may last for ten years. *M*A*S*H*, *Cheers*, *All in the Family*, *The Simpsons* and *Taxi* spring to mind; *Seinfeld* lasted for nine seasons and change (the first season was just four episodes). Note that those shows produced only twenty-two episodes a season. Allen came up with thirty-nine—and for the first ten seasons, his shows were an hour long! And while it's true that Jack Benny, Bob Hope and George Burns enjoyed longer careers because they also succeeded in TV, the witticisms of those long-lasting comedians were devised by a phalanx of gag writers, whereas Allen, a phalanx unto himself, wrote the bulk of his shows solo.

But while radio was his oyster and in television he failed in a variety of formats, his literary voice, which he began to find in the early thirties in pieces written for *Variety, Judge, College Humor* and the fledgling *The New Yorker*, continued to flower in random essays and speeches. Thus, when the public, which had made him a durable success on radio, rejected him on television, and the pundits pronounced him washed up, Allen turned out *Treadmill to Oblivion*, a captivating memoir of his radio days. Straightaway he emerged as a humorist. *Much Ado About Me*, a wise and witty autobiographical account of his vaudeville days, followed, validating his new status as a literary humorist of the first rank. It is no big stretch to suggest that had he not died (at sixty-two) and lived to continue writing, Allen might have joined Mark Twain, Ring Lardner, Josh Billings, and James Thurber in the Pantheon.

♦ ♦ ♦

Fred Allen entered this world on May 31, 1894, in a shabby Irish enclave on the fringe of Boston, billed as John Florence Sullivan. His mother died before he was four, whereupon his father, a low-paid, boozing bookbinder, consigned him to Lizzie Herlihy, a money-strapped maiden aunt, who raised the boy in a boardinghouse she ran for indigent family members.

Johnny Sullivan's formal education ended upon graduation from a so-called commercial high school, which prepared young men of the lower classes—those ostensibly without the talent, ingenuity or intelligence to move into the higher echelons of the executive ranks—to acquire simple skills, such as typing and bookkeeping, which would serve them as they went into the world to eke out a living. But during those school years, he was a stack boy at the Boston Public Library (from ages fourteen to seventeen) where he read every book on humor at hand. Meanwhile at home he practiced the juggler's art.

From the time he did his juggling act at a library employees' party and was showered with applause, he took off for the life of a performer and never looked back. His first appearance in public was at age sixteen in a Boston amateur contest. The following year he became part of a professional amateur troupe for 50 cents a night. When a heckler called out, "Where did you learn to juggle?" the skinny kid snapped back, "I took a correspondence course in baggage smashing." The resulting laughter was ambrosia to young Sullivan, who immediately added a comic monologue to his act. Starting at age eighteen, the tyro juggler-cum-ventriloquist-cum-banjo player-cum-clarinetist-cum-comic monologist worked one-nighters and split weeks, performing for people in small towns all over America, a self-described nomad—"part gypsy and part suitcase"—initially billed under his given name, Johnny Sullivan. Later, due to the vagaries of vaudeville, he was also booked as Paul Huckle, Freddy St. James—and at age 21, on a tour of Australia, his billing read:

> "Freddy James, The World's Worst Juggler—
> His Patter Whilst Juggling Is Very Humorous."

Traveling for eleven months by train and slow boat in Australia and New Zealand, the lad avidly studied between engagements works of the classic humorists, English humor magazines, and scores of joke books, the basis for his encyclopedic knowledge of jokes and comedy. He later wrote, "I [went] to Australia a juggler, and . . . return[ed] to America a monologist."

Back home other comedians paid him for material (he created the famous "Guzzler's Gin" routine, a mainstay of Red Skelton's act), while he worked his way up to premier bookings. The twenty-five year old had a smashing debut in 1919 at the celebrated Palace Theatre (the nadir, he wrote, recalling his youthful vaudeville tours, "was the kind of theatre so far in the backwoods the manager was a bear. He paid the acts off in honey. *Field & Stream,* not *Variety,* reviewed the acts"). He soon achieved Broadway stardom as a comedian, followed by escalating success in a series of musical comedy revues, for which he also wrote sketches (and in one of which he met Portland*, who was a dancer).

In show business circles he became known for his fast, savage wit. Joe McCarthy, editor of *Fred Allen's Letters,* writes: "It was while he was appearing . . . in Toledo on a dreary Christmas Day that Allen ad-libbed perhaps his most famous, widely plagiarized wisecrack. The orchestra leader was a gloomy little man who never laughed as he listened to Allen's witticisms during three shows a day. Finally Allen could stand the musician's unsmiling acidity no longer. Leaning across the footlights, he asked, "'What would you charge to haunt a house?'"

While he toured in the mid-twenties in "The Greenwich Village Follies," Allen wrote a regular column, gratis, for *Variety* called "Near Fun," with items like these:

> The height of deceit—a bald man wearing
> a toupee when he calls on his mother.

♦ ♦ ♦

> The Automat is the first restaurant to
> make it possible for the poor man to
> enjoy food served under glass.

---

*Named by her antic father after Portland, Oregon, where she was born.

Poem
Hush little bright line
Don't you cry
You'll be a cliché
Bye and bye.

And these fictional news items, forerunners of what, eighty years later, sustain the publication *The Onion.*

Passé News

Liverpool, England—American dramatic actor leaves the country. Being left-handed, the actor found it impossible to keep replacing monocle in right eye.

Butte, Mont.—Glass blower with carnival was stricken with hiccups and blew 100 percolator tops before he could stop.

Layoff, Fla.—Old actor who retired to start raising rabbits has gone out of business. Learned too late that the two rabbits he started with were brothers.

In 1932 Allen, then a Broadway star, was recruited for network radio, which was destined to last barely more than a generation. From the start, he was broadcast comedy's Columbus. Among the first of the vaudevillians to venture from the stage to the microphone, Allen boldly planted a flag on the shore, declaring this new territory free from formula and faintheartedness. The rest is a story of the transformation of the ex-juggler into a humorist.

Fred Allen was sui generis. He never met a cliché he didn't disdain; even avoided greeting friends by saying "hello." One downside of being totally original was the enormous amount of his material constantly lifted by others, among them Al Jolson, George Jessel, Milton Berle, Phil Baker and others who wantonly performed his routines as their own. But Allen, continually gushing comic ideas like a never-ending geyser, barely noticed. By the time they were using his stuff, he was resident on some distant comedy galaxy, unreachable by mere mortals. Another downside to his free-form style was the blue penciling by executive watchdogs whenever Allen mocked sacred cows, upsetting sponsors, organizations, entire cities.

While Allen made his name in the humor trade, he was also a serious thinker. He had a knowledge of what's important (among his notes: "favorite piece sculpture—the milestone nearest home"), and this is, conjecturally, the element that renders his comedy insightful.

Although Allen was one of the wittiest aphorists since Oscar Wilde, you will find only a few of his bon mots in *Bartlett's;* one in the 15th edition, two in the 16th. Previous editions managed to include lesser-known Allens, among them one William Allen, who in his seventy-six years on earth appears to have offered only: "Fifty-four forty, or fight!" To compensate for *Bartlett's* paltry selection, this book offers a gallimaufry of Fred Allen's epigrams, some familiar, many not. And to even the score, except for the citations directly above, you won't find another mention of *Bartlett's* herein.

Fred Allen was a contradictory character: fearlessly independent, compassionate, cynical, decent, droll, modest, tough-minded, irreverent, serious, honorable, driven, charitable (he supported needy relatives, tithed to the Catholic church, regularly handed out money to down-and-outers from his vaudeville days, as well as to strangers who knew of his reputation for benevolence). He owned neither car nor house, opting to live in rented apartments and hotels. He kept in touch with colleagues but abstained from industry schmoozing at events and parties, preferring the company of the uncelebrated. That he was universally liked is an anomaly of both celebrity and show business. Wilfrid Sheed, in his superb essay on W. C. Fields, "Toward the Black Pussy Cafe," reports that in the cutthroat vaudeville world, comedians sometimes threatened the lives of those who stole their material, concluding, "Very few kindly men can have emerged from vaudeville." Fred Allen was one.

In his introduction to *Low Man on a Totem Pole,* by H. Allen Smith (see complete text on pages 181–186), Allen wrote: "To Mr. Smith it is the little man, the neurotic nonentity, the tattered extrovert, the riff and raff whose lives are important. To those who slink through life fraught with insignificance he dedi-cates his pen. Mr. Smith is the screwballs' Boswell." The same may be said of Fred Allen. Consider, in this light, an aforementioned feature of his show, "People You Didn't Expect to Meet." Some of those he introduced to the nation were a worm entrepreneur, a spiritualism sleuth, a dog tailor, a subway poet, a pretzel bender, a parachute tester, and a bologna stuffer.

In the forties *The Fred Allen Show* was one of the two or three most listened to radio programs in America, number one in 1947 when he was the subject of a *Time* cover story. The most popular character on the program was a bumptious southern politician of Allen's invention called Senator Claghorn, who, whenever he uttered what he considered a witticism, invariably added his catchline, "That's a *joke,* son!" He drank only from a Dixie cup, and bellowed, "Ah'm from so far down south, mah family's still treadin' water in the Gulf of Mexico! That's a *joke,* son!" Claghorn, played by the extraordinarily talented Kenny Delmar, also the show's announcer, struck a chord in the national psyche, and a mere four weeks after his initial appearance, America had gone Claghorn-crazy.

I, then a nineteen-year-old U.S. Navy man of big dreams stationed at the submarine base in New London, Connecticut, was struck with an idea: I would create a comic strip based on Claghorn, become rich and famous, and never have to suffer the indignity of real work for the remainder of my life. In my bunk in the torpedo area aboard the U.S.S. *Spikefish*, I drew a series of cartoons of the senator. During my next "on liberty" day, I rode the New Haven train to Manhattan, found Delmar in the phone book, and showed him my creation. Delmar, saying rights to the character belonged to Allen, introduced me to the comedian at NBC headquarters in Rockefeller Center. There, I brazenly told Allen my plan (leaving out the rich and famous part).

That I was unqualified to create a syndicated comic strip did not deter me. Indeed, with the tacit understanding that I needed to observe the radio show as a basis for developing the feature, I became a V.I.P. guest each week at the live broadcast. It was enormously exciting for a kid like me, who loved radio comedy, to be in the audience in NBC's renowned Studio 8-H* at a live broadcast. This was before television; we never saw our radio idols, we only heard their voices. I vividly recall the exhilaration I felt to be breathing the same air as my hero! Before the broadcast started, Allen came out from behind the curtain, baggy-eyed, florid-faced, pompadoured, bow-tied. In that compelling voice tinted with the soft Rs and flat As of his native Boston, he said if we were there by mistake we still had time to get out before the show began, and promised us a military escort. But if we were determined to remain, he informed us that a stifled laugh does not die when you put it back in your

---

*Constructed to lure Arturo Toscanini from Italy to America to conduct the specially formed NBC Symphony Orchestra, and home to *Saturday Night Live* since that show's inception.

throat. It lives in your lower colon to laugh at the food as it passes through. The studio audience went nuts. When the red light signaled ON THE AIR, we were his. Even though all we saw was a group of ordinary-looking people standing in front of microphones holding scripts, we instinctively knew something spectacular was happening.

And what a group! Allen, his force of energy overwhelming, his wife Portland Hoffa, and his band of actors (for whom he custom-tailored the material), a sound effects man, and the singing De Marco sisters—with the band seated behind.

It was a theatrical event—the insouciant comedian, slitty eyes dancing with mischief, as famous as your male movie idols—Gable, Grant, Bogart, Gary Cooper—doing his stuff right there in the same room with you, *for* you. True, those iconic leading men were jut-jawed handsome (in Bogart's case, snotty-curled-lip handsome) and hard-muscled, (unlike the thick-waisted, baggy-faced Allen). Still, Fred had the edge; he worked in the present, in the moment, he wasn't merely an arc light image beamed onto a movie screen. He was *there!* He was drop-dead *funny,* not merely joke-funny. He was funny deep in his cells. That was the key.

Sure, those movie heroes could win the dame, come out of barroom brawls standing, shoot (blanks) to kill guys in black hats . . . but they couldn't make you *laugh.* Breathtaking! The famed comedian, live, on a high wire, with no net, deftly wielding jokes—his balance pole—entertaining millions, the ultimate pro, supremely confident, carefree, relaxed, having a fine time, schpritzing with verbal swagger, revealing no signs of the constant border skirmishes with network nitpickers who bedeviled him (see *The Little Men,* page 6). The program drew solid laughter, explosive whenever Allen fired off an ad-lib, breaking up his cast, then having to mentally edit the rest of the program, timed to end at an immutably fixed moment.

This added to the *frisson* that made the atmosphere in the studio crackle.

There was the time Allen interviewed a British falconer, one of those "People You Didn't Expect to Meet." The falconer brought along his eagle. The eagle, flying about the studio, unexpectedly departed from the script, shocking the hapless audience. Hysteria reigned. The laughter was loud and it was wild and it was sustained. Allen, forced to maintain equilibrium despite the startling turn while keeping his eye glued to the relentless progression of the big red second hand on the studio clock, nimbly improvised a side-splitting play-by-play of the unanticipated event, which became radio legend (see page 39).

Once, after a show, I brazenly handed the great comedian a page of comedy material and said, "Mr. Allen, I wrote you some jokes." "Son," he replied, "bringing a joke to me is like bringing a fender to Henry Ford." Another time, when I drew a caricature of him accentuating the pouches under his eyes, he was more benign, signing it, "Fred Allen, the man with the bags."

I never produced the comic strip, though years later I sold to King Features Syndicate one based on another writing comedian, Woody Allen (no relation). Nevertheless, after I was discharged from the service the following summer, Allen put in a word for me with someone at Eagle–Lion Studio who had signed Delmar to star in a Claghorn film called *It's a Joke Son!* (it wasn't). I hitchhiked to Hollywood to serve as Delmar's stand-in, altering my dream of becoming a rich, world-famous comic strip artist to rich, world-famous movie star.

One evening at dinner in Delmar's poolside suite at the fabled Chateau Marmont, he showed me a cautionary letter about the film colony from Allen, who, like Don Marquis's "archy," the cockroach, famously typed his correspondence in lower case (because, he claimed, "i have never been able to shift for myself "). The letter said, in part:

> *all the sincerity in hollywood you can stuff*
> *into a flea's navel and still have room left over*
> *to conceal eight caraway seeds and an agent's heart.*

I was astonished by the polish of that hard, little brilliant (which I instantly committed to memory, and dined out on for years after, and, as you will have noticed, appropriated for the title of this book). Until that moment, I had worshipped Allen simply as the one who made me laugh the most when I listened to him on our family Philco radio.

How This Book Came to Be

Cecily Truitt, co-owner of a Manhattan TV production company, was the inadvertent catalyst of this enterprise (which fact she will discover only when she reads this account):

One day in early 1997 I was pitching to Ms. Truitt and her staff a concept for an educational children's TV series. To my suggestion that we might engage a live animal as co-host, she demurred: "I love animals as much as anyone, and I've probably filmed more of them with children than anybody my age. But they cause problems because they tend to do unexpected things." I said that reminded me of the time Fred Allen had an eagle on his radio show, which caused a furor when it misbehaved during a live broadcast. Her face went blank. "Fred who?"

"You've never heard of Fred Allen?"

"I don't believe so."

I was stunned that a clearly intelligent person in broadcasting had never heard of my Radio Days idol. "Did your parents listen to the radio?" I asked. She said they did. I tested her on Jack Benny and Bob Hope, Edgar Bergen, Burns & Allen, Fanny Brice, Fibber McGee. She'd heard of them all. "I have to talk to your parents," I said. Her father was deceased but her mother, Alice, lived in Boston. I ordered Ms. Truitt to call her mother.

She glanced nervously at her staff around the conference table. "Now?"

I assured her this was important and urgent. "Mom," she said into the phone, "I'm here with a man who's appalled that I don't know the name of some guy who was on the radio. I'm gonna put you on the speakerphone to talk to him, okay?" She pressed a button on the phone.

"Alice," I said, "I have sad news. Your daughter has never heard of Fred Allen."

"*That,*" said Alice, "drives a stake through my heart!"

I asked Alice if she remembered how he sounded. She said she thought so. I pinched my nose and offered a couple of Allen's witticisms in a fair imitation of his gravelly voice. Alice laughed in the right places, and when she rang off, I told her daughter the story of Allen and the eagle.

In the days following, I felt a pang that The Great Man didn't exist for this media-wise young woman, which indicated that this deprivation would also hold true for others born after, say, Carnera flattened Sharkey, or the Dionne quintuplets commanded the world's attention. And the idea was born for a book to introduce Fred Allen to people too young to know about him.

This is that book.

It's a selection of Fred Allen's prose writings, correspondence, radio scripts, speeches, essays and penseés, some droll, some dark, some insightful, but none with soft, chewy centers. In addition to the comic stuff, the book contains material from a hidden compartment in Allen's soul, a treasure trove of discernment absent from his radio writing due to the various demands of having to please a sponsor and a network and appeal to a mass audience. Still, in his radio writing, there is always evident the literary sharpshooter's eye for the *bon mot*, and fairly esoteric language. On which other comedy show would you have been likely to hear "Filth and offal dance on this sea of scum," "buskin," "transcendentalist" (see Orson Welles sketch, beginning on page 26)? Yet while the radio work may strike our twenty-first century sensibility as a bit tame, be mindful that it was written anywhere from five to seven decades ago—and was, for its time, truly groundbreaking. That Allen was the creator of hundreds of radio shows between 1932 and 1949, providing the most literate comedy in the history of broadcasting under restrictions of strict censorship (he wrote: "if radio ever gets a Pulitzer Prize, it will be pinned to the censor's wastebasket") was a gift of immeasurable value to the dispirited multitudes of that glum time.

The material herein is but a sample of his extensive oeuvre. Some of it comes from the Allen family's private collection, some from his books, some from formerly unseen materials from the Fred Allen archive in the Rare Book & Manuscript Division of the Boston Public Library, where the Allen papers, tapes of his radio shows and objects of memorabilia reside, indicated in the card catalog simply as MS 2033. The collection, occupying twenty-seven feet of shelf space, reposes inside acid-free gray boxes containing numbered folders tagged by subject. Among the riches are thousands of handwritten pages bearing Allen's tiny hieroglyphics in stubby pencil on scraps of foolscap, habitually carried in his coat, folded into quarters which he pulled out to scribble on when a notion popped into his mind. These jottings, sometimes no more than a word or two, many inscribed in a personal shorthand which makes them appear incomplete, were later transcribed into ledgers that became source books from which he would mine and polish comic bits for his radio program. (Allen longed to be a writer of material which would be bound into books, rather than merely of words which were sent out into the ether to disappear. In 1942 he vowed: "if i get chased off the air i will start writing and perhaps have peace of mind for the first time in ten years.")

Allen once said: "all humor is a matter of opinion."

Herewith my opinion: Fred Allen was funny. I know, because he makes me laugh.*

And that is the ultimate test.

---

*See *Woody Allen,* by Eric Lax, Knopf, 1991, page 285 for verification of my credibility in this matter.

"all the sincerity in hollywood . . ."

SELECTIONS *from the* WRITINGS
of RADIO'S LEGENDARY COMEDIAN

fred allen

radio

From the program of March 23, 1947.

ALLEN—Tell me, Mr. Moody, is there any invention you wish had never been made?
MOODY—I could do without the radio.
ALLEN—The radio, eh?
MOODY—I don't hold with furniture that talks.

Allen's first program, a half-hour show called Linit Bath Club Revue, *went on the air on Sunday, October 23, 1932, over the Columbia Broadcasting System. On March 31, 1934, the show, under the name* The Hour of Smiles, *was extended to one hour, which, three months later, became* Town Hall Tonight. *This meant Allen had to come up with twice the amount of comedy material. Finally, the show was cut back to a half-hour format. In* Treadmill to Oblivion *Allen recalls that event as part of his overall work schedule.*

ON JUNE 28, 1942, from midnight to 1 A.M. we did our final full-hour program. Ours was the last of the comedy hour shows in radio. Times had changed. Costs had increased and the salaries of the stars who could attract audiences had risen so high that an executive mentioning an actor's salary was risking a nosebleed in conference. Many of the half-hour shows had been reduced to fifteen minutes. The hour shows had completely disappeared or had been halved to thirty minutes. When the Texas Company decided to do a half-hour program the next October it took a load off my mind. I knew how a baldheaded man felt after removing his toupee on a hot day.

For eight years, 39 weeks each year, we had written and performed a 60-minute program. The first show was done in New York, from 9 to 10 P.M., for the Eastern audience. Three hours later we did a repeat show. (The use of transcriptions was unknown at that time.) A repeat show meant just that. Our cast had to return to the studio at midnight and repeat the entire program for the audience in California and the West Coast.

The work involved in writing and assembling a weekly radio show began to seem like a recipe for a nervous breakdown. During the early years it was fun. At this point it was drudgery. I was reading nine newspapers a day looking for subject matter for jokes, topical ideas we could use for news vignettes, unusual characters we could interview on "People You Didn't Expect to Meet," motion picture and play reviews to check, pictures and stage shows we could burlesque and whose stars we might book as guests. Walking along the street, riding in cabs or on the subway, I always had my head in a newspaper or magazine. Every few minutes I was tearing some item out of something and stuffing it into a pocket. As the day wore on my pockets seemed to be herringbone goiters and I looked as though I was a walking wastebasket.

The following vignette from Town Hall Tonight, *December 30, 1936 (plus others in the "politics" section), exemplifies how Allen incorporated items of popular culture into the show.*

ALLEN—Radio City, New York. With the coming of the New Year the Town Hall News looks back on 1936. While newspapers and other radio programs bring you the high-lights of the past year . . . The *Town Hall News* brings you the lowlights. Tonight we present a parade of nobodies. A cavalcade of simpletons whose inconsequential activities during 1936 meant absolutely nothing!

(Fanfare)

ALLEN—Chicago, Illinois. On April first Ramrod Dank invented a negative craze that swept the county. Presenting the first man to coin a Knock Knock in 1936, Mr. Ramrod Dank!

DANK—Is it safe to come out?

ALLEN—Yes, it's all right.

DANK—I been hidin' since Labor Day.

ALLEN—I don't wonder. How did you come to start the Knock Knock fad, Mr. Dank?

DANK—I dunno. I was sittin' in the house alone and some-body knocked on the door. It came to me like a flash and I says "Who's there?"

ALLEN—Could you give us your first knock knock?

DANK—Sure. Knock knock.

ALLEN—Who's there?

DANK—Noel Coward.

ALLEN—Noel Coward who?

DANK—*(Sings)* I'm a Noel Coward Hand from the Rio Grande.

In the first years of the radio show, Val Eichen, a friend from vaudeville, sent Allen his reactions. Allen wrote this letter to Eichen when Eichen took ill. The radio comedians mentioned are Eddie Cantor and Joe Penner, who both came to radio from vaudeville around the time Allen did. Rattray, Publisher of the Easthampton (L. I.) Star, *was a mutual friend of Allen's and Eichen's.*

may 2
1934

dear val..

comrade rattray has written me in code about your indisposition. i have tried to decipher the code without much success so i am still not sure just what is going on.

i know that you have been a rabid allen fan for nearly three years and i have always been afraid that something would happen to you on that account. if you have been going abroad shouting allen praises you have possibly aroused the ire of a cantor fan. this is dangerous business, mr. eichen.

cantor fans are easily aroused and their fury knows no limitations. if a cantor fan takes a dislike to you you are apt to be ptomained in a delicatessen . . . send your suit to a tailor and have it come back with a crease in the pants running around the side of the leg . . . find a stale blintz in your mailbox or otherwise undergo some other experience equally embarrassing.

i told you some time ago that if you thought the programs were okay to keep it under your hat where the discovery would have company in the form of dandruff . . . i felt that the world would eventually learn that i was on the air and then the cantor fans could worry as to how the news got out. if you think a penner or cantor admirer put a pill in your beer to bring on your ailment, i wish you would let me know.

i can get revenge for you easily. simply by sending a couple of stale jokes to either of these fellows i can make them the laughing stock of the air. a stale joke would sound new in most of their routines and once their listeners had tasted a new gag they would demand more and then these merry andrews would have cause for worry. they have been reading almanacs to their listeners for many months with no one the wiser. i have even heard their studio audiences laugh when the boys read weather reports. if they have had anything to do with laying you low through contaminating any liquids that it has been your wont to quaff say the word and i will get busy.

i hope that you will soon be about complaining about the quality of your radio entertainment and then i shall feel that you are normal again . . .

best for now and i hope you will soon feel better, sir.

fred allen

With the exception of Allen, radio comedians were free of interference by network censors. Their self-reflexive routines, too bland to offend, were cobbled together by teams of gagsmiths who sought little more than to make people laugh: Benny's stinginess, Fibber's messy closet, Fanny Brice's squalling Baby Snooks, Joe Penner's inane catch phrases, Cantor's six daughters, Bergen's obstreperous dummy, Hope's girlie jokes (sure-fire yocks before masses of GIs). This was the stuff that kept Hooper ratings high. Whereas to Allen, whose humor often contained references to prominent members, and significant events, of the passing scene, humorless network arbiters—suspecting in every quip ulterior motives that might incite litigation, pillory by the church, cancellations by sponsors— were an affliction determined to sandpaper his barbed observations. To say that Allen took umbrage at these bluenoses is a gross understatement. Indeed, many of his more acrid remarks were aimed at "echo men," "negative men," and "molehill men," terms of opprobrium with which he tarred his sponsors, their advertising agents, and network executives. One of the latter, who insisted on modifications in Allen's scripts, was designated by him as "vice president in charge of waving fingers at comedians." Of an ad agency that lobbied to remake his show along the lines of Show Boat, *a successful program, he said, "They kept trying to shove an eggbeater up my ass and make me a floating faux pas like* Show Boat." *He fought them to a draw, but paid in blood pressure.*

a vice-president in an advertising agency is a "molehill man." a molehill man is a pseudo-busy executive who comes to work at 9 A.M. and finds a molehill on his desk. he has until 5 P.M. to make this molehill into a mountain. an accomplished molehill man will often have his mountain finished even before lunch.

◆ ◆ ◆

echo men are very important in the world of advertising. they are men who follow in the wake of the big executive and echo his sentiments as they are expressed.

◆ ◆ ◆

an advertising agency is eighty-five percent confusion and fifteen percent commission.

The following piece is from Allen's radio memoir Treadmill to Oblivion.

THE LITTLE MEN

Within the hierarchy of the little men there is no man who can outlittle the minor executive in a large corporation who treats his authority as he treats a tight suit. In a tight suit he is afraid to make a move. With his authority the minor executive takes the same precaution. There are thousands of these negative men huddled in the places where minor executives conceal themselves in the labyrinths of the big corporations. They use the clam philosophy. If a clam never sticks its head out it is never overtaken by trouble. If a minor executive never commits himself he can never be cited for anything that has gone askew in the business. It was once rumored that fledgling executives walked around their offices backwards so they wouldn't have to face an issue. It was told that a freshman executive was found suffering from malnutrition lying on the floor in front of the elevator. He had been on his way to lunch and couldn't determine whether he should go up or down. He was afraid to make a decision.

We had men of this ilk in radio. The eternal aggravating factor stemmed from the fact that the actors lasted longer in the industry than the executives. There always seemed to be fresh clusters of miniature men making rules to get things on an efficient basis. As soon as the actors had adjusted themselves to this new regime the miniature men were no longer with the organization. A new pack of trivial fellows were loose in the company feeling their executive oats and making new rules to get things on an efficient basis.

Our program seemed to be forever caught in the tidal wave of executives being swept in and out of office. The new brooms in the organization would just make a sweeping decision and there we were standing in the dust. Each week, as soon as we had prepared our comedy script, all heck (the network censor does not acknowledge the existence of hell) would break loose. The process of creation is imposing form on something that has no apparent form. While we had the empty sheets of paper, and the show was nonexistent, the censor, the agency men and the sponsor were as quiet as a small boy banging two pussywillows together in a vacuum. However, the minute that we had imposed form on the nonexistent, the drones became men of action. When the script appeared, jokes had to be deleted, mention of competitive products and networks had to go and political references were banished lest they stir up somebody in Washington. During the war we could not mention the weather in New York City. The network minds claimed that U-boats off the shore could pick up our radio program. How it would help the enemy if the crew in a U-boat on the bottom of the ocean off Easthampton acquired the information that it was a rainy day in New York I could never quite understand. There were so many things in those days I could not quite understand, especially about low-level executive thinking.

There was one petty tyrant in the network whose ambition was to become a legend. With our help he finally made it. You probably do not recall the time that our program was cut off the air. At that precise moment you no doubt had your own troubles; but we were cut off. The newspapers highlighted the incident. The tyrant made a vague statement. We retaliated and had midgets picketing the network carrying signs reading "This network is unfair to the little man." Feeling, as it gained altitude ran high. Sides were chosen. Some favored the vindictive executive. Others the comedian.

This is the case history of the decision. With a comedy program it was always difficult to time the show exactly. If the audience was enthusiastic the laughter was sustained and the program longer. Since there was no way we could anticipate the audience's reaction, until the program was actually on the air, we had to arrive at an appropriate timing. For several weeks we had been running over, and the end of the show had been cut off abruptly. We had told a number of jokes about "our show [having] no end" and one week we started the program with the end of the previous show as a public service. This was to enable people to hear the end of the show they had been denied. Apparently we had been irking the despot. For weeks he must have been madly spinning around on his swivel. Finally, one week, as he read the new script, he decided to crush me under an iron memo. He issued a dictum, shouting up through the air conditioning so that every employee in the organization might hear his words. Unless certain material deriding network officials was deleted from the script he was going to cut our show off the air. We refused to eliminate something we thought harmless. He refused to dilute his disciplinarian pronouncement. If we did the lines, he would cut us off. We did. And he did.

The executive is no longer with the network. I am. If this is justice it is news to him.

These are the shocking lines that provoked the dilemma.

PORTLAND—Why were you cut off last Sunday?

ALLEN—Who knows? The main thing in radio is to come out on time. If people laugh the program is longer. The thing to do is to get a nice dull half hour. Nobody will laugh or applaud. Then you'll always be right on time and all of the little emaciated radio executives can dance around their desks in interoffice abandon.

PORTLAND—Radio sure is funny.

ALLEN—All except the comedy programs. Our program has been cut off so many times the last page of the script is a Band-Aid.

PORTLAND—What does NBC do with all the time it saves cutting off the ends of programs?

ALLEN—Well, there is a big executive here at NBC. He is the vice-president in charge of "Ah! Ah! You're running too long!" He sits in a little glass closet with his mother-of-pearl gong. When your program runs overtime he thumps his gong with a marshmallow he has tied to the end of a xylophone stick. Bong! You're off the air. Then he marks down how much time he's saved.

PORTLAND—What does he do with all this time?

ALLEN—He adds it all up—ten seconds here, twenty seconds

there—and when he has saved up enough seconds, minutes and hours to make two weeks, NBC lets the vice-president use the two weeks of your time for his vacation.

PORTLAND—He's living on borrowed time.

ALLEN—And enjoying every minute of it.

♦ ♦ ♦

Allen's speech upon receiving a Peabody Award—the "Oscar" for excellence in broadcasting.

Thank you very much. To me, this honor, while significant, is a little confusing. During the 12 years I worked in radio I was well-paid—I have the tax receipts from Mr. Morgenthau to prove it—but while I was on the air the Peabody Committee paid no attention to me. The minute I left radio I received this award. I still don't know whether the Committee is paying me a tribute for the work I have done in the past or whether the Committee is grateful to me for getting out of radio. Last year, while my program was off the air I won the Fordham College Poll. This year, while out of work, I have received a Peabody Award and an award from The Catholic University, at Washington. Next year, if I keep away from Hollywood, I will probably win an Academy Award.

When I read the headline in the *Times* saying that Mayor LaGuardia had won an award and then, under the Mayor's name, I saw my name in fine print, I thought that perhaps I was getting my award for listening to the Mayor's program. I think the Peabody Committee could save a lot of time and trouble each year by giving Mayor LaGuardia all of its awards. The Mayor covers everything in radio. His program is a happy blend of *Mary Margaret McBride, Information Please and Gangbusters.* One week, the Mayor will tell you how you can make mock french-fried potatoes with artichoke roots. The next week, he gives you the names of the bookmakers and hurdy-gurdy owners he has chased out of the city. The following week, the Mayor explains the City Budget to you so thoroughly that you know how many feet of hose the Fire Department has on hand and how many plungers the Sanitation Department is operating. The Mayor's radio program reports the news, it provides outstanding entertainment and educational features and I think it merits all of the Peabody Awards. I would like to suggest that since Mr. James Byrnes in his efforts to conserve fuel has stopped the Fireside Chats and instigated the curfew confusion—it might be a good idea to have the Mayor put his program on at midnight. This will not only provide entertainment but it will enable the people of New York to kill that extra curfew hour the Mayor presented to the City some weeks back.

But—getting back to my award—I think that every comedian in radio deserves some sort of an award. And I will tell you why. The way of the transgressor may be hard but the transgressor's path is a petal-strewn lane compared to the road the comedian traverses weekly on his way to the microphone. All humor is a matter of opinion and everyone in radio with enough authority to operate a memo pad has an opinion that jeopardizes the comedian's humor. The network has a censor, the advertising agency has a producer and the sponsor has a bustling vice-president who supervises the company's radio attractions. Until the comedian assembles his script, the censor, the producer and the vice-president are incapable of action. They lie dormant, contemplating their desktops, in their executive lairs.

But the minute the comedian has assembled his weekly quota of jokes and turned in his script, these guardians of sponsor, network and listener interests become fraught with interest and catapult themselves into action. To give you an idea of how these frustrated characters function—let us say that the comedian has a paragraph in his script that reads—"Jack Benny told me a great gag today. Jack said, 'The best way to keep a dead fish from smelling is to cut off its nose.'"

It seems like a very simple joke. Jack Benny says "The best way to keep a dead fish from smelling is to cut off its nose." Well, the script is sent over to the network censor. He pounces on the joke. Jack Benny is on an opposition network. The comedian can't mention Jack's name. The rest of the joke the network censor doesn't mind but Jack Benny's name has to come out.

Next, the comedian's script is sent to the advertising agency. The Producer reads what is left of the joke and hits the ceiling. The anti-vivisectionists are strong in this country. You can't cut a fish's nose off. Every anti-vivisectionist in America will be up in arms. The Hearst papers will start another campaign. The comedian tries to explain that the fish in the joke is dead but it doesn't help. The advertising agency producer is adamant. He insists that the fish was alive when it was caught and, as the gag reads in the script, there is no definite proof that the fish has succumbed to rigor mortis. The producer says it is a dangerous cross-reference, the anti-vivisectionist radio listeners must be protected and he deletes the reference to the cutting off of the fish's nostrils.

Now, the script goes to the sponsor's office. The vice-president in charge of radio is galvanized into action. Is the comedian crazy? A fish joke? The sponsor's brother sells WHAM a Spam derivative. Why should the sponsor let the comedian plug the fish industry, his brother's biggest competitor? If he makes people fish conscious the comedian will put the sponsor's brother out of the meat business. The vice-president removes the word fish which is all that remains of the original joke.

On the night of the broadcast the comedian arrives at the microphone. Instead of the hilarious fish gag he tells a dull joke about the housing shortage being so bad he went into a restaurant and couldn't even get a cottage pudding. The next day, 200 people who are living in trailers and old packing cases in defense areas around the country write anonymous letters to the sponsor saying that because he has made light of the housing shortage, the comedian is an isolationist, a saboteur and pro-Nazi. The sponsor sends for the comedian and the next week people tuning in the program find that the comedian has disappeared and the sponsor now has a new musical show featuring Guy Lombardo or Spike Jones and his City Slickers.

That is why, after 13 years of radio, Jack Benny's hair is snow white. That is why Edgar Bergen is as bald as Kate Smith's elbow. That is why Bob Hope jumps all over the country playing army camps where the network censor, the advertising agency producer and the sponsor's vice-president can't get at him. And that is why, Ladies and Gentlemen, I think that every comedian who survives in radio is entitled to an award. I thank you!

Radio Survey—Polls

PORT—Mama says your Hooper rating went down again.

ALLEN—The Hooper rating. That guy lives in a phone booth . . . He calls up a few people in a handful of towns and tells you how many radio listeners you have in the whole forty-eight states. It's like multiplying the bottom of a bird cage and telling you how many grains of sand there are in the Sahara Desert.

PORT—How low can you go in the Hooper rating?

ALLEN—Minus two.

PORT—Minus two?

ALLEN—That means that not only nobody listens to your

program but two people who don't hear it are going around knocking it.

◆ ◆ ◆

sketch—man escapes from hospital—brain removed—trace to radio studio—find asking for autographs.

◆ ◆ ◆

in radio . . . an original idea is community property in no time.

"Allen's Alley"

The most famous feature of the Allen show was a five-minute segment called "Allen's Alley," for which Allen created four proto-typical American types (he called them "vocal cartoons")— a southern politician, a Bronx housewife, a taciturn New Englander, and an urban Irishman. Each week, with the locale established by music and sound effects, Allen sauntered through the Alley, knocked on four doors, and asked a question based on some current topic.

The first door was that of Senator Beauregard Claghorn, the bigoted, booming-voiced, bumptious southern politician he created, whose real-life counterparts still exist.

Here's a sample of what the audience heard.

(Knock on door . . . Door opens)
ALLEN—Pardon me, sir.
CLAGHORN—Claghorn's the name. Senator Claghorn, that is. Stand aside, son! Don't hold me up! Ah'm busier than a flute player's upper lip durin' a rendition of William Tell.
ALLEN—You're busy?
CLAGHORN—Ah'm checkin' on that Hoover report.
ALLEN—What is that Hoover report, Senator?

CLAGHORN—Herby made a list of things he forgot to fix when he was President. He's givin' the list to little old Harry so's Harry can fix 'em now.

ALLEN—Fine.

CLAGHORN—Herby says the Army an' the Navy is wastin' money. The Army's throwin' money around like the taxpayer was the enemy. Ah found one item: the Army spent two billion dollars for fly swatters to send to Alaska. When the fly swatters got up there they found there wasn't no flies in Alaska.

ALLEN—They sent the fly swatters back?

CLAGHORN—Not the Army, son! The Army spent four billion dollars more to raise flies to ship to Alaska so's they could use them fly swatters. That's how the Army works, son!

The second door Allen knocked on in "Allen's Alley" was that of Pansy Nussbaum.

(Knock on door . . . Door opens)

ALLEN—Ah, Mrs. Nussbaum.

MRS. N.—Nu, you were expecting maybe Ingrown Bergman?

ALLEN—Well, Mrs. N., today the telephone has been with us for fifty years. What is your reaction to it?

MRS. N.—Thanks to the telephone, today I am Mrs. Pierre Nussbaum.

ALLEN—Really?

MRS. N.—When I am a young girl, footloose and fancy, mine maiden name is Pom Pom Schwartz. Also, I am having two sisters: Caress and Ginger.

ALLEN—Caress Schwartz?

MRS. N.—Also Ginger.

ALLEN—Fine.

MRS. N.—Mine sisters are getting married. Caress is marrying Skippy Cohen.

ALLEN—I see.

MRS. N.—Ginger is marrying Leroy Berkowitz. He is doing well, a pickle salesman, specializing in odd lots, by ap-pointment.

ALLEN—And with both of your sisters married . . . ?

MRS. N.—Sam Cupid is passing me by.

ALLEN—You couldn't get a boy friend?

MRS. N.—I am washing everything in Lox. I am brushing with Pepsodent the teeth. I am taking by Arthur Murray dancing lessons. I am also learning magic tricks and using Mum.

ALLEN—And nothing happened?

MRS. N.—I am still a wallflower.

ALLEN—What finally happened?

MRS. N.—One day, mine father, Ziggy Schwartz, is putting in the house a telephone.

ALLEN—I see.

MRS. N.—On Halloween I am sitting home alone bobbing for red beets. Suddenly the phone is ringing—I am saying hello.

ALLEN—Yes?

MRS. N.—A voice is saying, "Cookie, I am loving you. Will you marry me?"

ALLEN—And you?

MRS. N.—Foist I am saying, "Positively!" Later, I am blushing.

ALLEN—And that is why you say . . .

MRS. N.—Thanks to the telephone, today I am Mrs. Pierre Nussbaum.

ALLEN—But why be so grateful to the telephone company?

MRS. N.—They are giving Pierre a wrong number . . .

Note that this material was written for the ear not the eye, to be spoken by the voices of Allen's versatile acting company, employing their timing and attitudes—rather than to be read silently from a printed page. Still, the salty Allen flavor comes through. Allen was the only radio comedian who generously gave others all the punch lines. For a sense of his generous, minimalist technique, go back over the sketch above and read only Allen's speeches.

Other Pansy Nussbaum rejoinders (which affirm Allen's taste for puns).

ALLEN—Ah, Mrs. Nussbaum.

MRS. N.—Nu, you were expecting maybe Weinstein Churchill?

ALLEN—That's a pretty gown you have on.

MRS. N.—It is mine cocktail dress.

ALLEN—I didn't know you went to cocktail parties.

MRS. N—We are only living once. *N'est-ce pas?*

ALLEN—That is true.

MRS. N.—Why not enjoining? *C'est Levy.* Life is a deep breath. You are exhaling, it is gone.

ALLEN—Ah, Mrs. Nussbaum!

MRS. N—Nu, you are expecting maybe The King Cohen Trio?

ALLEN—Ah, Mrs. Nussbaum!

MRS. N—Nu, you are expecting maybe The Fink Spots?

ALLEN—Ah, Mrs. Nussbaum!

MRS. N—Nu, you are expecting maybe Cecil B. Schlemiel?

ALLEN—Ah, Mrs. Nussbaum!

MRS. N—Nu, you are expecting maybe Rudyard Kaplan?

At the ballet, Mrs. Nussbaum liked the shapirouettes.

After Mrs. Nussbaum, Fred called on New Englander Titus Moody.

ALLEN— . . . I think I'll start for "Allen's Alley."

PORT—What is your question tonight?

ALLEN—This week the Better Business Bureau is completing its 25th year of service. Thousands of cases of fraud in real estate, stocks and other get-rich-quick schemes, have been prosecuted. And so our question is—Have you ever been swindled by a disciple of sharp practice?

PORT—Shall we go?

ALLEN—As the man said when his wife grabbed his money at the racetrack—"You bet."

("Alley Music" . . . Orchestra)

ALLEN—Ah, here we are back in "Allen's Alley," Portland. . . . I wonder if Mr. Moody is still up.

(Knock on door. Door opens)

PARK—Howdy, Bub!

ALLEN—Tell me, Mr. Moody, have you ever been the victim of a fraud?

PARK—Only once.

ALLEN—What happened?

PARK—Well one time I had to go up to New York to buy some new sports jackets for my scarecrows.

ALLEN—I see.

PARK—I was gimpin' up Broadway with a big wad of money in my shoe.

ALLEN—Uh-huh?

PARK—A feller wearin' a checkered suit and a jazz-bow tie pulled me into a doorway.

ALLEN—I see.

PARK—He says, "Charlie. How'd you like to have security in yer old age?"

ALLEN—Security?

PARK—He says—"Charlie, How'd you like to own yer own toll bridge?"

ALLEN—Your own toll bridge?

PARK—"When they're comin' across," he says, "they'll be comin' across fer you."

ALLEN—You fell for it?

PARK—I took off my shoe and gave that oily cuss all my money.

ALLEN—For nothing?

PARK—He gave me a blue uniform, a whistle, a rockin' chair and a collapsible turnstile.

ALLEN—A turnstile, eh?

PARK—He took me to a bridge. It was uptown a hundred and seventy-five streets.

ALLEN—175th Street. That's the George Washington Bridge.

PARK—I set up my turnstile, sat back in my rockin' chair, and started blowin' my whistle to collect my tolls.

ALLEN—What happened?

PARK—Cars kept shootin' by me. Nobody stopped to pay nothin'.

ALLEN—You were on the New York side?

PARK—Ayar.

ALLEN—What did you do?

PARK—When I closed up my turnstile fer lunch I walked to the other end of the bridge.

ALLEN—Uh-huh.

PARK—I seen right away what the trouble was.

ALLEN—What was the trouble?

PARK—Three fellers with turnstiles at the other end was collectin' all the tolls.

ALLEN—At the Jersey end.

PARK—It only goes to prove.

ALLEN—To prove what?

PARK—If you're thinkin' of openin' a toll bridge across the Hudson.

ALLEN—Yes?

PARK—Don't open up on the New York side.

ALLEN—You mean the money is all at the other end?

PARK—Yep. People will pay anything to get out of Jersey— So long, Bub.

(Door slams)

The last house in "Allen's Alley" was that of Ajax Cassidy, an im-bibing, hypochondriacal Irishman, a type Allen knew well from his Boston youth.

ALLEN—And that brings us to Mr. Cassidy's shanty. I wonder what is happening Chez Cassidy tonight.

(Knock on door. Door opens)

AJAX—What's all the fiddle-faddle? Who's instigatin' the din? Oh . . . How do you do?

ALLEN—Well, Mr. Cassidy. How are you tonight?

AJAX—Terrible, terrible, terrible . . . *(Coughs)* I'm not long for this world.

ALLEN— . . . Tell me, Mr. Cassidy, what about this used car business?

AJAX—We're livin' in an age of high pressure. People are

hounded into buyin' cars with slogans. There's a Ford in your future.

ALLEN—I see.

AJAX—Where I'm goin' in the future, a Ford won't help. What I need is a fire engine. With an asbestos hose.

ALLEN—Uh-huh.

AJAX—The Pontiac is the Most Beautiful Thing on Wheels!

ALLEN—What's wrong with that?

AJAX—The most beautiful thing on wheels is Maureen O'Hara on a bicycle.

ALLEN—I see your point.

AJAX—Ask the man who Owns One.

ALLEN—That's Packard.

AJAX—Have you ever tried to talk to a man in a Packard?

ALLEN—No.

AJAX—Ask the man who Owns One. He won't even answer you.

ALLEN—Don't you ever use an automobile?

AJAX—After many years of contemplation, during which I have studied the various means of transportation and weighed their merits pro and con, I have arrived at one conclusion.

ALLEN—And what is your conclusion?

AJAX—That it is best for me to restrict me travel to one type of vehicle.

ALLEN—And that is . . . ?

AJAX—The station wagon.

ALLEN—The station wagon?

AJAX—Every Saturday night when they take me away to the station . . .

ALLEN—Yes?

AJAX—They send the wagon. Good-by to ye, boy!

(Door slams)

The Feud with Jack Benny

"jack benny's so cheap, he'd put his finger down a moth's throat to get his clothes back."

♦ ♦ ♦

"jack benny couldn't ad-lib a belch at a hungarian banquet."

♦ ♦ ♦

Allen wrote of the blandness of early radio, which he set out to shatter:

Radio in the '30s was a calm and tranquil medium. Oleaginous-voiced announcers smoothly purred their commercial copy into the microphones enunciating each lubricated syllable. Tony Wons was cooing his soothing poems. Bedtime stories were popular. Radio was one unruffled day from Cheerio in the early morning through to Music to Read By at midnight. Radio was fraught with politeness. No voice was ever raised in public.

Waggishly setting out to "ignore precedent" on his program of Wednesday, December 30, 1936, Allen departed from his written script, took a good-natured potshot at his friend Jack Benny, and accidentally started a faux feud that served both comedians well for a decade. It happened, a week after Benny, on his show, bragged about his prodigious talent on the violin, that Allen had as a guest ten-year-old Stuart Canin, a violin prodigy from Long Island. The boy played a piece titled "The Bee" (not Rimsky-Korsakov's "The Flight of the Bumblebee" as has been erroneously codified in numerous books, nor Dvorak's "The Bee" as Jack Benny claimed in his memoir). This "Bee" was composed by one Francois Schubert, a little-known Alsatian, whose name is also confused with the other F. Schubert. As the applause died down, Allen ad-libbed:

ALLEN—That was the Bee, Mr. Benny, played by a ten-year-old boy. Why, Mr. Benny, at ten you couldn't even play on the linoleum. If Mr. Benny had heard this tyke's rendition of the Bee he should hang his head in symphonic shame and pluck the horsehairs out of his bow and return them to the tail of the stallion from which they had been taken . . . Benny is the only violinist who makes you feel the strings would sound better back on the cat's intestine.

As Allen had correctly assumed, Benny was listening, and on his show the following Sunday night, after firing a few shots at Allen in retaliation, he said he would be happy to render the same song on his program the instant any music lover requested it. Having heard this, Allen, on his next show, said:

ALLEN—I would like to respond to some verbal mayhem shunted at me, from Hollywood on Sunday last, by an itinerant vendor of desserts [Benny's sponsor was Jell-O]. I won't mention this gelatin hawker's name at the moment. Suffice it should be to say he has a sideline, called by some, a radio program. On this program, last Sunday evening, this gentleman . . . and the word *gentleman* is used with intent to libel . . . this spoilsport fell asleep . . . fell asleep on his own program, mark you, making it unanimous . . . while he was asleep he had a dream . . . during which . . . this defiler of the Stradivarius . . . shot at me six times. That same night I ate a Welsh rarebit and what I didn't do to him in my dream is nobody's business. All I said originally, Ladies and Gentlemen—was that Mr. Benny couldn't play the Bee on his violin. Last Sunday, he had a cold. Colds are caused through vitamin deficiency proving that Mr. Benny hasn't even got a Bee in his vitamins. Plied with aspirin, and reeking of menthol, he swore that he would play the Bee on his program next week. This dire news has seeped into every nook and cranny of the country. What effect will this solo have on contemporary life in America, Mr. Kut Priceler* the eminent violinist says:

JOHN—If Jack Benny plays the Bee next Sunday, it will set the violin back 20 years.

DOUG—My husband and me live in a trailer, our radio's in the car. If my husband turns that radio on next Sunday . . . I'm cuttin' the trailer loose . . . with me in it . . . and hopin' for the best.

ALLEN—Mr. Lemuel Randypone . . . Southern Planter . . . says:

CHAS—If Benny plays his violin next Sunday the cotton crop is saved. The South will be all ears. And the ears will be stuffed with cotton.

ALLEN—Max Raucous . . . prominent union organizer . . . says:

HARRY—If somebody can get this Benny to put his violin down on a chair before Sunday, will I start a sitdown strike, and How!

ALLEN—When these are but a few of the opinions voiced, during the week, Ladies and Gentlemen, it is small wonder we look forward to Sunday next with apprehension. Tonight . . . in order to stunt Mr. Benny's growth we have brought back to the microphone the young man who made this whole argument possible . . . Master Stuart Canin. . . . As you perhaps know, Stuart, your rendition of the Bee has caused a modicum of trouble . . . Mr. Benny is in a spot . . . He is supposed to play the Bee next Sunday and I

*In the final script Allen crossed out Fritz Kreisler and penciled in this name.

thought if we wanted to be fair about the whole thing you and I could explain to Mr. Benny how he can manage it. You know . . . we can tell him how to hold the violin and everything. Now, you show me how to hold it and I'll tell Mr. Benny. Oh yes! The violin is held in the left hand, Mr. Benny. The little finger resting lightly on the first string. The round end of the violin sets back into the neck . . . a little over to your left . . . with just a dash of Adam's apple peeking around the corner. The bow . . . or crop . . . as you cowboys probably call it, Mr. Benny, is held in the right hand. Now . . . to play the violin what do you do Stuart? I see . . . you scratch the bow across the strings. Fine. And now that Mr. Benny knows how to hold the violin little ten-year-old Stuart Canin will show little thirty-five-year-old Mr. Benny how to play the Bee. All right, Stuart.

(Violin solo)

ALLEN—Thank you, Stuart. That was "The Bee" Mr. Benny. And on Sunday next we wish you well.

The following statement was penciled out of the script.

Next Sunday, Ladies and Gentlemen, the world will realize that Aesop spoke 2000 years too soon when he said . . . "Nero fiddled and Rome burned, if Jack Benny fiddles on Sunday . . . America will burn." I rest my case!

Benny, despite having promised to play "The Bee" on his program, for weeks didn't, claiming his violin was lost. Allen offered a reward for return of the instrument to Benny, who in turn, hired a detective to find it. When Benny's fiddle mysteriously reappeared and he played "The Bee" on his show, Allen responded:

ALLEN— . . . that solo did more for the aspirin industry than the last flu epidemic . . . I have never heard such wailing and squalling since the time two ghosts got their toes caught in my ouija board. Of all the foul collections of discord foisted on a radio-loving public under the guise of music, that herd of catcalls took the cake.

Allen summed up the feud in Treadmill to Oblivion:

Jack and I heckled each other for many seasons and eventually made a picture together called *Love Thy Neighbor.* The feud did do two things—it improved Jack's violin playing: he told me later that he had to practice for months to be able to play "The Bee" on his program; and the association with Jack increased our listening audience greatly.

Guest Stars

Celebrities flocked to appear on Allen's show, anticipating the sheer fun of playing in sketches based on themselves, a style Saturday Night Live *successfully employs. Orson Welles had been a twenty-five-year-old wunderkind when he directed, produced, starred in—and took credit as co-writer of—*Citizen Kane, *his first film, widely considered one of the greatest of all time. Welles, a Renaissance man, was already celebrated for writing, producing, directing, and starring with The Mercury Theatre (which he also founded) on stage and in radio (his 1938 "The War of the Worlds" panicked the nation into thinking we were being attacked by invaders from Mars; his 1937 radio version of* Les Misérables, *which Allen satirizes here, was an unequivocal triumph). Larger than life, Welles was a prodigious international presence.*

PORTLAND—Who is your guest?

ALLEN—That's my trouble. I had a telegram from Orson Welles saying he wants to see me tonight.

PORTLAND—Orson Welles!

ALLEN—That's the way I feel about it, too. What he wants to see me—

(Knock at door)

PORTLAND—That's Orson Welles! *(Shrieks)*

ALLEN—Portland, control yourself! Come in!

(Door opens)

ALLEN—Yes?

TECHNICIAN—Is this the microphone Mr. Welles is going to use?

ALLEN—Yes, this . . .

TECHNICIAN—Step aside buddy. One! Two! Three! Woof! Woof! Hello, Max! One, Two, Three, Woof, Woof. Hello, Max!

ALLEN—Just a minute, friend. What is this?

TECHNICIAN—I'm Mr. Welles's personal chief technician.

ALLEN—And you check . . .

TECHNICIAN—Right. This microphone might be all right for a Schnook like you, but for Mr. Welles it's gotta be perfect. One, Two, Three, Woof, Woof. One, Two—

(Phone rings)

TECHNICIAN—That phone's for me. It's Max; Max is my superior.

ALLEN—Anybody would be your superior.

TECHNICIAN—Hello, Max? Right, Max. I should report to Mr. Welles it's okay. Okay, Max.

ALLEN—All right, if you're through . . .

TECHNICIAN—Wait a minute. What's these scratches on the microphone?

ALLEN—Our Announcer, Mr. Godfrey, has buck teeth.

TECHNICIAN—I hope Mr. Welles don't notice it.

ALLEN—Do you think I should spray the microphone with perfume?

TECHNICIAN—With you around, it wouldn't hurt none, brother.

(Door slams)

ALLEN—Orson Welles. Special technicians he has to have, to go on the air. All the President needs is two logs and a Boy Scout.

PORTLAND—I'm getting scared.

ALLEN—Why?

PORTLAND—Maybe Mr. Welles is coming here to get even with you.

ALLEN—Even for what? I had nothing to do with *Citizen Kane.*

PORTLAND—I know. But you told all those jokes about Orson Welles.

ALLEN—That was last year. What can he do . . .

(Knock at door)

PORTLAND—Orson Welles! *(Shrieks)*

ALLEN—Portland! Quiet! Come in!

(Door opens)

SISSY—Excuse me. I shan't be a minute. *(Calls)* Hello out there! *(Louder)* HELLO, OUT THERE! *(Louder)* HELLO, OUT THERE!!!

ALLEN—Look, brother . . .

SISSY—Quiet, please. *(Coyly)* Hello, out there!

ALLEN—What is this?

SISSY—I am Mr. Welles's personal acoustical diagnostician.

ALLEN—Oh.

SISSY—I'm testing the acoustics.

ALLEN—I see.

SISSY—If Mr. Welles doesn't like the acoustics you may have to tear down part of the studio. *Ta-ta!*

ALLEN—We should wreck the building. Stop trembling, Portland.

PORTLAND—But I'm scared.

ALLEN—Don't be silly. If Mr. Welles is coming up here about those jokes I told about him last year, why should I worry? I've never seen a genius with muscles yet. If he wants to start . . .

(Knock at door. Door opens fast)

ALLEN—Now what?

DOCTOR—*(Sniffs three or four times)*

ALLEN—What's with this sniffing, Mister? Who are you?

DOCTOR—I'm Mr. Welles's personal physician. *(Sniff . . . Sniff)*

ALLEN—But what . . .

DOCTOR—I'm checking the air in here to see if it's fit for Mr. Welles to breathe. *(Sniff . . . Sniff)*

ALLEN—Everybody else is breathing this air.

DOCTOR—Mr. Welles is a great artist; he's a very sensitive man.

ALLEN—Sensitive . . . He was on Benny's program last Spring. If he can stand that he can stand anything.

DOCTOR—Mr. Welles had a cold that night. Good bye!

(Door slams)

PORTLAND—Mr. Welles sure doesn't take any chances, does he?

ALLEN—I wish I knew what he wanted to see me about. I'm getting nervous myself now.

(Knock on door . . . fast. Door opens)

ALL—*(Hum of voices)*

ALLEN—Hey, wait a minute, you guys.

STAGEHAND—*(fast)* Beat it, Bud. Slim! You and Mike roll that red plush carpet from Mr. Welles's car right to the microphone.

MIKE—Okay.

STAGEHAND—Sam! Have you got your trumpet ready for the fanfare?

SAM—Standin' by, sir.

ALLEN—Look, fellers.

STAGEHAND—Will you get out of the way. Slim! Light the incense and get the spotlights ready.

SLIM—Okay.

SAM—Mr. Welles is stepping out of his car.

STAGEHAND—For Pete's sake! Hurry with that rug.

ALLEN—Here, let me help!

SAM—Mr. Welles is entering the building.

STAGEHAND—Hit those spotlights!

ALLEN—Get that rug down.

SAM—Mr. Welles is here.

STAGEHAND—The fanfare, Sam! Presenting . . .

(Fanfare by orchestra)

ALL—Mr. Orson Welles!

(Applause)

ALLEN—Well, good evening, Mr. Welles.

ORSON—Excuse me. *(Tests mike)* One, two, three! Woof! Woof! Hello, Max!

ALLEN—The microphone has been tested, Mr. Welles.

ORSON—Good. *(Calls)* Hello, out there! Hello, out there!

ALLEN—The acoustics have been checked, Mr. Welles.

ORSON—Good. *(Sniffs three or four times)*

ALLEN—The air has been approved.

ORSON—Very good. I'm a busy man.

ALLEN—I know.

ORSON—I am very happy to be here on the Philip Morris Program this evening.

ALLEN—That was Friday night.

ORSON—Oh, yes. What night is this?

ALLEN—Sunday. This is the Texaco Star Theatre. My name is Allen.

ORSON—Fred Allen?

ALLEN—Yes.

ORSON—How do you do, Mr. Allen?

ALLEN—Mr. Welles, I'm thrilled . . .

ORSON—Naturally. I'll come to the point, Mr. Allen. Last year, on your program, you said several derogatory things about me.

ALLEN—Oh, I say, you haven't met Portland yet, Mr. Welles. She's dying to meet you. Portland!

PORTLAND—Yes.

ALLEN—Portland, this is Orson Welles.

ORSON—Hello, Portland.

PORTLAND—*(Screams. Runs away)*

ORSON—What's the matter with that child? Was that a shriek?

ALLEN—No. She has asthma—it's pitched high.

ORSON—Well let's get down to business, Mr. Allen. About those derogatory remarks . . .

ALLEN—I don't recall.

ORSON—Do you remember what you said about my home in Hollywood?

ALLEN—No. I don't.

ORSON—Perhaps I can refresh your memory. You were talking about those trick doorbells they have out in Hollywood.

ALLEN—Oh, those fancy chime effects.

ORSON—Yes. You said when a person rang my doorbell

sixteen peacocks flew out of a transom, a man in a belfry in the hall pealed his bell, twenty-one guns went off in a salute, and I came out of four doors simultaneously.

ALLEN—I must have been stuck for a joke that night. I don't remember.

ORSON—And that time you were discussing Hollywood Victory Gardens. What was it you said?

ALLEN—I just said that all you did was go out to your back yard, point to the ground and say "Grow!" and fourteen acres of corn sprang up. I'm sorry if you . . .

ORSON—Well, that was last year. I'm here to speak to you about this year.

ALLEN—Mr. Welles. Believe me. I haven't made a single crack about you this year. I wasn't even planning to. I swear it.

ORSON—What's the matter, Fred? Don't you like me any more?

ALLEN—You're not mad, Orson?

ORSON—Not at all, Fred. I enjoy a good laugh as well as anybody.

ALLEN—Well, Orson, this is a great surprise to me.

ORSON—Why, Fred?

ALLEN—I always pictured you as a man from another planet, a transcendentalist, a genius, a legend in the making—and here you are joking and laughing with little old egg-laying me.

ORSON—Fred, I wish somebody would do something about this Superman myth the public has swallowed about me. It's embarrassing. After all, I'm just an ordinary guy.

ALLEN—I know, Orson. But your early life has been shrouded in mystery. If people were told something about your childhood they would know you are not a cross between Flash Gordon and a Quiz Kid. You're just another man in the street.

ORSON—What's there to tell, Fred? I was born in Chicago. Like any other kid I went through grammar school. And at the age of five I entered Northwestern University.

ALLEN—At five you entered college?

ORSON—As a sophomore. I skipped the freshman year. My college days were uneventful. I majored in Esperanto . . .

ALLEN—I see.

ORSON—Well, I got out of college at seven, *magna cum laude.* I hung around with Einstein for awhile. We tiffed one day over a bit of calculus. I rejected Einstein's theory. At the age of twelve I resigned from the Smithsonian Institute and went into the theatre.

ALLEN—And the rest is history.

ORSON—It's been nothing, Fred. So I've had a little success in the theatre, radio and pictures. Does that mean I'm a genius? I wear the same clothes as other men, I eat the same food. And like any ordinary guy who works hard, my feet hurt at the end of the day.

ALLEN—No wonder. Trying to squeeze fourteen toes in an ordinary pair of shoes. But, tell me, are you back from Hollywood for good?

ORSON—No, I'm just giving Hollywood a short breathing spell.

ALLEN—Are you going to do a play in New York?

ORSON—I don't think so, Fred. Broadway seems to be stressing burlesque this season, and I can't see myself doing a strip tease.

ALLEN—You can't tell. Gypsy Rose Welles. Or a Shakespearean revival, All's Welles That Ends Welles.

ORSON—No, Fred. I'm going back into radio for the

Lockheed Company. That's really why I wanted to talk to you tonight.

ALLEN—About your new program?

ORSON—Yes.

ALLEN—If I can give you some hints, or introduce you to Ma Perkins, I'd be . . .

ORSON—No, Fred. I'm getting along in years. I have finally come to the conclusion that I can no longer carry on alone. I need a co-star. An actor with a flair for the buskin. A man with dramatic distingué. An artist who can match my dramatic ability.

ALLEN—You have found such an actor, Orson?

ORSON—Yes, Fred. You!

ALLEN—Me, Orson? Gad, this is an honor. What is your first play?

ORSON—We'll do Victor Hugo's great story, *Les Misérables*. You will co-star with me.

ALLEN—Just you and I do the entire play?

ORSON—It'll be fifty-fifty. I'll play Jean Valjean.

ALLEN—And I?

ORSON—You will play the French detective, Javert.

ALLEN—Javert, eh? *Je suis ze law.*

ORSON—Oh. Do you speak French, Fred?

ALLEN—Just enough to get out of Rumpelmayers, Orson.

ORSON—That will help a lot. If we can rehearse a minute we'll run over the play here before I go.

ALLEN—Okay. We'll present our co-starring epic, *Les Misérables* . . . Allen and Welles. Gosh! . . . Are you ready, Orson?

ORSON—Yes, Fred. You have your part?

ALLEN—Yes. Frankly, I'm a little nervous.

ORSON—You'll be all right, Fred. You're with me in every scene.

ALLEN—We're co-stars.

ORSON—Yes. Everything is fifty-fifty.

ALLEN—How does the play start?

ORSON—I'll do the narration, Fred. I have to set the scene. Can I have some appropriate music?

ALLEN—You bet! Mr. Goodman, appropriate music for Mr. Welles, please.

ORCHESTRA—*(Heavy dramatic music . . . Fades)*

ORSON—*(Dramatic)* *Les Misérables!* Victor Hugo's immortal story of a soul transfigured and redeemed, through suffering. This is an Orson Welles production.

REED—Radio version of *Les Misérables* prepared by . . .

ORSON—Orson Welles!

REED—Directed by . . .

ORSON—Orson Welles! During Orson Welles's presentation of *Les Misérables,* Mr. Welles will be assisted by that sterling dramatic actor of stage, screen and radio, Mr. . . .

ORCHESTRA—*(Heavy dramatic music . . . Fades quickly)*

ALLEN—Hold it! Hold it! Wait a minute, Orson.

ORSON—Is something wrong, Fred?

ALLEN—All I've heard so far is Orson Welles. If I'm co-starring at least my name should be mentioned.

ORSON—I announced you, Fred. The music cut in too quickly.

ALLEN—Watch that, Mr. Goodman. I have a public, too, you know. Mr. Welles, I'm no bit player. You have your Mercury Theatre, but don't forget, I've been a star with the Mighty Allen Art Players for a decade.

ORSON—I wish you wouldn't be so impulsive, Fred. *Les Misérables* is the story of two men, Jean Valjean, the hunted convict, liberated after serving nineteen long years in the galleys—and Javert, the merciless minion of the law. You're on Jean Valjean's trail all through the play.

ALLEN—I'm Javert and you are Jean Valjean.

ORSON—That's right. Each character is equally important to the story. It's fifty-fifty.

ALLEN—Okay. Let's go.

ORSON—The first scene is a dingy garret in the slums of Paris. As the story opens I am hiding out. I think I have escaped you. As we first see Jean Valjean he is soliloquizing.

ORCHESTRA—*(Heavy dramatic music . . . Fades)*

ORSON—*(Dramatic)* At last, Jean Valjean, you are safe. There is no cause to fear this Javert who has hounded you so long. His fearful instinct which seemed to have divined the truth, that had divined it. And which followed me everywhere. That merciless bloodhound always in pursuit of me, is finally thrown off the track, absolutely baffled. *(Dramatic laugh)* But hark! That sound upon the stairs! Those footsteps! Those same plodding footsteps!

(Knock at door)

ORSON—Javert! What is to be done? Ah, this window! Jean Valjean will never be taken! Good-by, Javert!

(Knock at door)

ORCHESTRA—*(Heavy dramatic music . . . Fades)*

ALLEN—Hey, wait a minute, Orson.

ORSON—Later, Fred. We start the second scene now.

ALLEN—Well, never mind the second scene. What about that first scene?

ORSON—Why, it was fifty-fifty.

ALLEN—But you took both fifties.

ORSON—That's ridiculous, Fred. You stole the whole scene.

ALLEN—I did?

ORSON—What broke up Jean Valjean's soliloquy? What caused him to leap through that open window?

ALLEN—I . . .

ORSON—It was that knock on the door. And who knocked on that door? Javert.

ALLEN—Javert. I play Javert.

ORSON—You motivate the entire story. If you hadn't knocked at the door I'd still be in the garret. We'd have no play.

ALLEN—Oh.

ORSON—In this second scene you steal the whole thing. I'm just a foil.

ALLEN—A foil. That sounds good. What is the second scene?

ORSON—It's years later. This time you, Javert, have me trapped. Cosette Fabantou, a demimonde, is concealing me in the back room of a bistro. I, Jean Valjean, am pacing up and down.

ORCHESTRA—*(Heavy dramatic music . . . Fades)*

COSETTE—*(French)* Jean! Will you stop pacing? *Toujours* up and down.

ORSON—This is the end, Cosette, my farewell to freedom. Instead of liberty waits the galley crew, the iron collar, the chain at my foot—fatigue, the dungeon, the plank bed—all the horrors I know so well. To be tumbled about by the jailer's stick. To have my bare feet in iron-bound shoes. To submit morning and evening to the hammer of the roundsman who tests the fetters. Time is short, the net is tightening.

(Police whistle)

ORSON—Javert!

COSETTE—Quick, Jean Valjean, through this trapdoor.

ORSON—Merci, Cosette! Jean Valjean will never be taken again. Au revoir, Javert!

(Police whistle)

ORCHESTRA—*(Heavy music . . . Fast fade)*

ALLEN—Hold it! Hold it! Now look, Orson . . .

ORSON—Fred, you were magnificent.

ALLEN—I was . . .

ORSON—You stole that scene right out from under my nose.

ALLEN—I stole the scene again?

ORSON—Gad, that suspense, man.

ALLEN—Suspense? Aw . . . I . . .

ORSON—I've seen Javert played a hundred times. The Theatre Guild, The Grand Guignol, Eddie Dowling have played Javert. But I've never heard a Javert get the tone out of that police whistle that you got tonight.

ALLEN—Look, Orson, I don't want to hog the thing, but in act two all I've done is knock on a door and blow a whistle. After all, I'm an actor, not a soundman. When do I get to read some lines?

ORSON—The next scene is all yours, Fred. Your speech is the climax of the entire play.

ALLEN—Now we're getting someplace. What's next?

ORSON—In this final scene you trail me through the sewers of Paris. You finally corner me, single-handed, there we stand, face to face—I have just a few words and then you speak.

ALLEN—I speak. Good. Let's go!

ORCHESTRA—*(Heavy music . . . Fades)*

ORSON—*(Dramatic)* Mon Doo! Alone in this sewer! Trapped like a rat who crawls through the night in this hideous muck of the city. The gloomy darkness, this narrow archway above my head, these two slimy corridor walls. Sluice as far as the eye can see. Filth and offal dance on this sea of scum. But hark! That sloshing through the muck. Javert! At last you've cornered me, Javert! Don't talk, Javert! Before you seal my doom, I would speak for the last time.

You will never take Jean Valjean alive, Javert. *(Laughs)* The water in this sewer is rising, Javert. I am six feet nine. You, Javert, are five feet two. The water rises, Javert. There is no turning back. The water—higher—higher . . . now, Javert, you have Jean Valjean at your mercy. Pronounce my doom. Speak, Javert. Speak.

ALLEN—*(Gargles water and tries to talk)*
ORCHESTRA—*(Music up to finish)*

Allen gave his opinion of the Welles sketch in a note to writer H. Allen Smith.

nov. 9th
1942

h.a.

the program is still a pain in the iliofemoral ligament. the orson welles show was the only one i have liked. it is hard to take a guest each week and make the thing jell. the time is short, ideas cannot be worked out and we generally end up with a few gags and an anemic sketch that stems from some activity that concerns the guest. orson was a lot of fun. i had never met him before but the impression i had conjured up of the genius was all dissipated. he is a jolly man about glass and in our meetings was regular in every respect. i would not hesitate to propose him for membership in the woodman of the world, grange number 7, boothbay harbor, if he cared about joining this worthy order . . .

People You Didn't Expect to Meet

In this feature Allen interviewed people with silly occupations. Among these was a British falconer who brought an eagle to the program on March 20, 1940. Allen's report of the incident is from

Treadmill to Oblivion. *His reply to the disapproving NBC executive, which appears at the end, was copied and widely circulated throughout the broadcast-advertising community.*

One of our guest stars was responsible for probably the loudest and longest laugh ever heard on radio. The laugh lasted for over forty minutes. Its reverberations may still be echoing among some of the ancient acoustics of NBC. Here is how it happened.

I had read a piece in *The New Yorker* making mention of the arrival in this country of a British lecturer. He sounded quite interesting. His name was Captain Knight, and the subject of his lecture was "Falconry." We visited Captain Knight in his hotel quarters and found him chaperoning an ominous-looking eagle named Mr. Ramshaw. Captain Knight agreed to appear on our program bearing eagle.

This interview ensued.

ALLEN—Captain . . . I wonder if you could have Mr. Ramshaw give us an example of his flying prowess.
CAPTAIN—Yes. I think perhaps he might enjoy a short flight around the stage here, Fred.
ALLEN—Fine, could he carry my script around with him?
CAPTAIN—Why your script, Fred?
ALLEN— . . . It's no novelty for a comedian to see a script get the bird. But when a bird gets a script . . . We'll make radio history, Captain.
CAPTAIN—Very well. I shall have Mr. Ramshaw fly around the stage and land back on that bandstand. Ready, Ramshaw? Go.
(Bird flies around stage and lands)
ALLEN—Excellent. A perfect three-claw landing. . . . Good night and thank you, Captain Charles Knight.

That was the way it was supposed to end—but Captain Knight and I never did finish this interview. At rehearsal . . . the eagle seemed to understand. In the empty studio, Mr. Ramshaw took off from the Captain's wrist, spread his wings, flew a few feet and grounded himself on top of the bandstand. We tried it several times. Things went smoothly. Mr. Ramshaw even appeared to be enjoying himself.

That night, as the program progressed, everything was fine until Captain Knight read his line, "I shall have Mr. Ramshaw fly around the stage and land back on that bandstand. Ready, Ramshaw? Go!"

And Ramshaw went. He took off from the Captain's wrist gracefully but when he got aloft the glare from the brass instruments in the orchestra (the orchestra had not been at rehearsal) apparently confused him. He couldn't seem to locate the bandstand. He started flying around the studio, his talons clawing the air ad-lib. Women were shrieking, afraid that Ramshaw would light on their heads and descalp them. Captain Knight augmented the bedlam by rushing around the studio shouting pertinent instructions in his British accent to the eagle, who was busy wheeling over the audience giving an impression of a buzzard in a moment of indecision. As though he wanted to get as far away from the turmoil as possible, Ramshaw perched on top of a high column up near the ceiling. The imbroglio caused him to forget even the cruder points of etiquette. Mr. Ramshaw gave visual evidence that he was obviously not a housebroken eagle. The visual evidence fortunately just missed the shoulder of a student who had come down from Fordham University to advise me that I had won a popularity poll at the school. He was sitting on the stage after having presented me with a plaque earlier in the show.

As the audience laughed and shouted, the program carried on. Captain Knight was remonstrating with the eagle and advising him to come down from his lofty haven. In one pocket the Captain carried a few chicken heads for emergencies and to sustain Mr. Ramshaw during the day. As he pleaded with the eagle, the Captain started to wave a chicken head as a sort of grisly reward if Ramshaw would abandon his prank and return to captivity. Chaos was in bloom—the Captain with his British hullabaloo, the audience screaming with laughter, the women squealing with fright. Jokes were told, songs were sung, commercials were read. Nothing was heard.

The program went off the air on a note of sustained pandemonium.

After the excitement had become passé noise, I received a note from an NBC executive taking me to task for instigating this huggermugger. The executive received this reply:

march 25th
1940

dear mr. royal . . .

am in receipt of your letter commenting on l'affaire eagle as they are calling it around the young and rubicam office.

i thought i had seen about everything in radio but the eagle had a trick up his feathered colon that was new to me. i thought, for a minute, i was back on the bill with lamont's cockatoos.

an acolyte from your quarters brought news to us, following the nine o'clock broadcast, that the eagle was to be grounded at the midnight show. it was quite obvious that mr. ramshaw, as the eagle is known around the falcon lounge at the audubon society rooms, resented your dictatorial order. when his cue came to fly, and he was still bound to captain knight's wrist, mr. ramshaw, deprived by nature of the organs essential in the voicing of an audible complaint, called upon his bowels to wreak upon us his rebuttal to your martinet ban.

toscanini, your house man, has foisted some movements on studio audiences in 8 h, the bulova company has praised its movement over your network but when radio city is being torn down to make way for another mcguiness restaurant, in years to come, the movement that will be recalled by the older radio fans will be the eagle's movement on wednesday last. if you have never seen a ghost's beret you might have viewed one on mr. rockefeller's carpet during our stellar performance.

i know you await with trepidation the announcement that i am going to interview sabu with his elephant some week.

yours for a wet broom in 8 h on wednesday nights.

fred allen

In a recap of the event on the following week's show, Allen had this exchange with orchestra leader Peter van Steeden.

PETER—The eagle got more laughs than you did.
ALLEN—I could get laughs if I could use the same devices he did.

In 1948 a juggernaut called Stop the Music *derailed* The Fred Allen Show. *American radio listeners, happy recipients of Allen's gift of humor since 1932, were seduced away from his show by a different kind of gift—the chance to win cash prizes if they could answer musical questions on the phone. Allen offered to pay $5,000 to any listener who missed a call from the quiz show while tuned to his program. This didn't help his ratings, but he extracted laughs out of the situation nonetheless, with Jack Benny as his guest. The sketch, based on Benny's iconic persona of parsimony, unwittingly predicted the demise of Allen's program in precisely the way it happened the following season.*

(Door opens)

GUIDE—This is studio 8-A, folks.

ALLEN—Say, wait a minute, wait a minute . . .

GUIDE—This last booth is the control room.

ALLEN—Say, wait a minute.

GUIDE—That little man with the mildew on him is a Vice President.

ALLEN—Say, wait a minute. What is this?

GUIDE—This is a Radio City 60-cent tour. Okay, folks, let's get going . . . hey, wait a minute! I got a stowaway here!

ALLEN—A stowaway in a tour?

GUIDE—Only fifteen people paid. Now I got sixteen.

ALLEN—Who would be low enough to sneak into a tour to save sixty cents?

GUIDE—There's the guy. Hey, you!

JACK—Who . . . me?

ALLEN—Jack . . . Jack Benny!

(Applause)

ALLEN—Jack . . .

GUIDE—Come on! I'm gonna get sixty cents out of you if I have to . . .

JACK—Take your hand off my tie!

GUIDE—Come on!

JACK—Put me down!

ALLEN—Yes, guide, put Mr. Benny down. I'll give you the sixty cents.

JACK—Wait a minute, Fred. Wait a minute. Put that money away.

ALLEN—But Jack . . .

JACK—I've only seen half the tour. Give him thirty cents.

ALLEN—Here you are, guide.

GUIDE—*(Moving away)* Thanks. Follow me, folks. Now on your right is a water cooler.

(Door closes)

JACK—Well, Fred, it was nice of you to pay that thirty cents.

ALLEN—Oh, it was nothing.

JACK—"Nothing," he says. Thirty cents.

ALLEN—Jack, how can you be so cheap?

JACK—Oh, all right. Go ahead. Be like all the other radio comedians. Tell some cheap jokes. Say I'm tighter than the skin on Sidney Greenstreet's hip. I squeeze a nickel so hard the "E Pluribus" laps over the "Unum." Tell 'em.

ALLEN—Well, Jack, I didn't . . .

JACK—Oh, start insulting me, after I made a special trip up here just to say goodbye before I leave for Hollywood.

ALLEN—Well Jack, I . . .

JACK—All of a sudden I'm cheap. I won't even eat in the sun: my shadow might ask me for a bite.

ALLEN—Your shadow has teeth? Jack, don't get excited. Look, if you're cheap, you're cheap.

JACK—That's the way I look at it. Some people save asparagus ends, it's a hobby. My hobby is not spending.

ALLEN—Look, Jack, if there ever was a time you and I should not argue, this is the time.

JACK—What do you mean this is the time?

ALLEN—Well, a lot of—haven't you heard? A lot of the radio programs that have been on for many years have been cancelled. They'll not be back on the air next fall.

JACK—Well that's radio, Fred. It's dog-eat-dog. I always say only the fit survive.

ALLEN—Oh, how true. By the way, you finished tonight, didn't you?

JACK—Yes siree. Tonight was my last show of the season.

ALLEN—Did your sponsor mention anything about your program coming back in October?

JACK—Well, no, no, Fred. But we have a mutual understanding. You see, we always sort of take it for granted.

ALLEN—Oh.

JACK—The season ends, the sponsor shakes hands with me, and then we . . . yipe!

ALLEN—Jack! Jack, what's wrong?

JACK—Tonight he didn't shake hands.

ALLEN—Well . . .

JACK—But Fred, why should my sponsor want to get rid of me? Why, I'm funnier than I was when I started. And I'm getting less money . . .

ALLEN—Let's face it, Jack, radio needs new blood. Who knows, we may be through.

JACK—I've been in radio fourteen years. They can't throw me aside like an old shoe . . .

ALLEN—But Jack . . .

JACK—Fourteen years. And now, like an old shoe . . .

ALLEN—Well, Jack, you know how it is in radio. Today you're a star. Tomorrow Ralph Edwards is hitting you in the face with a pie.

JACK—Like an old shoe.

ALLEN—Well, cheer up, Jack. At least we have our memories. We've known each other for thirty years . . . we were in vaudeville, remember? You were doing a musical act.

JACK—Playing the violin. What a finish I had. When I played "Glow Worm" my violin lit up.

ALLEN—With those neon strings it was beautiful.

JACK—Remember, I'd put the bow in my teeth . . . and play "Listen to the Mockingbird?"

ALLEN—And as you played, two mockingbirds flew out of the back of your pants.

JACK—I stopped every show with it . . .

ALLEN—Ah, those were the happy days. The next time I saw you, you were just going into radio.

JACK—Radio. I remember the morning Marconi called me up.

ALLEN—Marconi?

JACK—Marconi and Singin' Sam—had a little radio station in a doorway down on the East Side. The antenna was a Western Union boy holding a wire . . .

ALLEN—Well, it's all over Jack. We've come to the end of the rainbow . . .

JACK—Seems like only yesterday I ran into the May Company and said, "Mary, stop demonstrating that Brillo."

ALLEN—Cheer up, Jack. When you're retired you can tune in on my program.

JACK—Your program? You mean you're not getting thrown out of radio, too?

ALLEN—Well, why should I?

JACK—Listen, if my program is old stuff, you with that broken down "Allen's Alley" . . .

ALLEN—Well now wait. I mean my new show.

JACK—New show?

ALLEN—People don't want entertainment today. A radio show has to give away things. Nylons, iceboxes, automobiles . . .

JACK—You mean, to stay on the air, you have to give things away? Free?

ALLEN—Yes!

JACK—I'll die first.

ALLEN—Well, not me. I'm auditioning my new program tonight.

JACK—And you're . . . Fred, you're giving things away?

ALLEN—Tons of stuff!

JACK—To strangers?

ALLEN—What's the difference who gets it?

JACK—Well, Fred, as long as I'm here in the studio . . .

ALLEN—Oh no, I'm sorry, Jack. Professional people cannot

participate—it's the rule.

JACK—But don't you ever find people on these programs changing their names to get something for nothing?

ALLEN—Well, occasionally we do catch a phony, but we're on the air—what can we do?

JACK—Nothing. You have to give them the merchandise?

ALLEN—That's right.

JACK—Hmm . . .

ANNOUNCER—Mr. Allen, we're ready for your audition.

JACK—Uh, I'll run along, Fred. So long.

ALLEN—So long, Jack.

JACK—Hmm. Giving away things for nothing.

(Door closes)

ALLEN—Well all right . . . Let's try out my new show.

　　(Trumpet fanfare)

ANNOUNCER—How would you like to be King for a Day?

(Cheering and music—"We're in the Money"—5 secs. then fade)

ANNOUNCER—*(Over music)* And here he is—the man who will change one of you nobodies into King for a Day—the old Kingmaker himself, Fred Allen!

(Cheering)

ALLEN—Thank you, thank you *(Cheering out)*—and good evening. Did all of you folks in the audience like those thousand dollar bills you found on your seats when you came in?

(Cheering)

ALLEN—Good. And if you want more, there'll be a big bag of money at the door. On your way out help yourselves. But the stage is loaded with hundreds of presents for the first man to answer our Jumbo Jackpot Question. He will be King for a Day. And here is our first eager contestant. Good evening, sir. What is your name? . . .

JACK—Myron Proudfoot.

ALLEN—Myron Proudfoot? You look like a chap I know.

JACK—I'm not interested in your friends. Start giving things away, brother . . . make with the question.

ALLEN—All right. Who was the sixth President of the United States?

JACK—John Quincy Adams.

ALLEN—John Quincy Adams is correct—and Mr. Myron Proudfoot is King for a Day!

(Cheering and music—"Pomp & Circumstance"—3 secs.)

ALLEN—Folks, here he is, King Proudfoot. Well, your majesty, how do you feel?

JACK—Never mind how I feel. What do I get?

ALLEN—First, for his majesty from . . . Tiffany's, this chromium pitchfork . . .

JACK—*(Excited)* Gee! A four-pronger! And it's all mine! . . .

ALLEN—This is just the beginning, King . . . a saloon and bartender to go with it; 4000 yards of dental floss, practically new; two floors of the Empire State Building; twelve miles of railroad track and a roundhouse completely furnished . . .

JACK—*(Excited)* I just keep pinching myself to believe it!

ALLEN— . . . a shovel, plus twenty unhampered minutes in the basement of Fort Knox . . .

JACK—I'm King for a Day!

ALLEN—And that's not all.

JACK—There's more?

ALLEN—Yes. We're going to start right now to make you look like a king. Sam, of Sam's Super Shoe Shine Stand, is here to brush your shoes. All right, Sam.

JACK—Sam, watch out for the buttons!

ALLEN—Next, the president of the Busy Bee Hat Cleaners is here to block your hat. Take the King's hat, Mr. Bumble.

JACK—And change the newspaper in the hatband.

ALLEN—Your suit is a little baggy, King. Boys, take his majesty's coat off.

JACK—Wait, wait . . .

ALLEN—On our stage we have a Hoffman pressing machine.

JACK—Now wait a minute! Wait a minute!

ALLEN—An expert operating the Hoffman pressing machine will press your trousers . . .

JACK—Now wait!

ALLEN—Take Mr. Proudfoot's pants off, boys.

JACK—Now wait! Wait a minute, Allen!

ALLEN—Keep your shirt on, King!

JACK—You bet I'll keep my shirt on!

ALLEN—We're a little late, folks. Tune in again next week . . .

JACK—*(Over Fred)* Oh, come on, Allen, give me my pants!

ALLEN—Quiet, King!

JACK—Allen, where are my pants?

ALLEN—Benny, for fifteen years I've been waiting to catch you like this.

JACK—Allen, you haven't seen the end of me!

ALLEN—It won't be long now!

JACK—I want my pants!

(Applause)

From a May 11, 1945, letter.

dear t. j. [smith]

 i am supposed to give up the program this fall. the doctor has told me that my blood pressure continues to rise and that unless i take a prolonged rest he feels that i will invite a chronic condition. i am planning to abandon the show after june and go to hollywood to make a picture in the fall. if i avoid the weekly aggravation that goes with the writing and the accumulation of the weekly rubble my pressure may go down and another day i may be able to return to the microphone as fresh as the proverbial daisy. there may be a little trouble with the sponsor but the cemeteries are full of men who didn't know enough to quit and i may establish a precedent if i leave at the height of my success. the word height here is used loosely. i fear that i have passed my peak despite anything you may have read in dr. pitkin's book "life begins at forty."

♦　♦　♦

Allen summed up his program in Treadmill to Oblivion.

Its epitaph reads Born October 23, 1932, as THE LINIT SHOW—Died June 26, 1949, as THE FRED ALLEN SHOW. The program might have enjoyed a few more years on borrowed time but my blood pressure was getting higher than the show's rating and it was a question of which one of us would survive. I did, a mortician friend assures me.

Television was already conducting itself provocatively, trying to get radio to pucker up for the kiss of death. Young men with crew cuts were dragging TV cameras into the studios and crowding the old radio actors out into the halls. Even without the coming of television radio seemed doomed. Year by year the survey figures showed a gradual shrinking of the mass listening audience. The audience and the medium were both getting tired. The same programs, the same comedians, the same commercials—even the sameness was starting to look the same.

Radio was the first free entertainment ever given to the public. Since it was piped into homes it was a service similar to running water. When the novelty of the shows wore off many people had more respect for running water than they did for radio. A house owner who would never think of speaking disrespectfully of the water in his house would rant around his radio set, sounding off about the dubious merits of some program he had just heard.

Radio could not survive because it was a by-product of advertising. Ability, merit and talent were not requirements of writers and actors working in the industry. Audiences had to be attracted, for advertising purposes, at any cost and any artifice. Standards were gradually lowered. A medium that demands entertainment eighteen hours a day, seven days every week, has to exhaust the conscientious craftsman and performer. Radio was the only profession in which the unfit could survive. When television belatedly found its way into the home, after stopping off too long at the tavern, the advertisers knew they had a more potent force available for their selling purposes.

Comedy has changed with the coming of television. The radio listener saw nothing: he had to use his imagination. It was possible for each individual to enjoy the same program according to his intellectual level and his mental capacity. In radio, a writer could create any scene that the listener could picture mentally. In television a writer is restricted by the limitation imposed on him by the scenic designers and the carpenter. With the high cost of living and the many problems facing him in the modern world, all the poor man had left was his imagination. Television has taken that away from him.

There was a certain kind of imaginative comedy that could be written for, and performed on, only the radio. Television comedy is mostly visual and the most successful comedians today are disciples of the slapstick. Jack Benny, with his comedy show, has been a star in radio for more than twenty years. I am afraid that twenty years from today none of the crop of

TV comedians will be found cutting elementary didoes before the cameras.

We are living in the machine age. For the first time in history the comedian has been compelled to supply himself with jokes and comedy material to compete with the machine. Whether he knows it or not the comedian is on a treadmill to oblivion. When a radio comedian's program is finally finished it slinks down memory lane into the limbo of yesterday's happy hours. All that the comedian has to show for his years of work and aggravation is the echo of forgotten laughter.

♦ ♦ ♦

He wrote a succinct coda to this in a December 21, 1955, letter:

we did over 780 shows and most of the air waves that were pregnant with our jokes and clever lines finished up caught in the crotches of pigeons, sparrows and flamingoes who dared too far north.

My Aunt Lizzie

Allen's memoir, Much Ado About Me, *is a warm, wise and wonderful autobiography. Here is an excerpt from the first chapter.*

On May 31, 1894, the population of Cambridge, Massachusetts, was increased by one. On that day a son was born to James Henry Sullivan and his wife Cecilia Herlihy of that city. In Irish homes in those days there was no idle talk about the stork. When babies arrived in Cambridge they were expected. Poor mothers, who could not afford the luxury of a hospital bed, had their babies at home. On the appointed day, a relative or a friendly neighbor came in to take over the housework. Then the doctor drove up in his buggy, hitched his horse, and hurried into the house with his little black bag. Some hours later, looking a mite disheveled, the doctor walked slowly out the front door and drove away in his buggy; a tiny cry was heard from within the confines of the house. A baby had been born. That was all there was to it.

On May 31, then, this performance was given; the result was John Florence Sullivan. Two years later, on June 27, 1896, the performance was repeated. The doctor drove away again, another tiny cry soiled the neighborhood acoustics, and a second son, Robert, had joined James Henry Sullivan and his wife Cecilia.

One year later Cecilia contracted pneumonia and died.

James Henry Sullivan was left to face the world with his

two small sons. After the funeral the usual family councils were held; there was a noticeable lack of enthusiasm among my father's brothers and sister when it was proposed that he and his brace of embryo males join one of their households. Our destiny was finally settled when one of my mother's sisters offered to make a home for James Henry and "the boys," as my brother and I were called.

I was not three years old. I knew that my name was John Florence Sullivan. I knew that my father, my brother Bob, and I were living with my Aunt Lizzie. All these early years are a montage of early memories; a house that had grapevines all over the place, another house with a great field in back to play in, and a parlor in which a coffin lay. Through the glass covering at one end of the coffin I could see a man's face; the man was strangely still. Later I was told that the man was my Grandfather Herlihy. The first thing I recall distinctly is a short walk I took with my Aunt Lizzie. As the walk started I was five years old, and we were living on Bayard Street in Allston. My aunt escorted me to the end of Bayard Street and pointed me towards a red brick building directly across the road. I scurried away, went through the open door, and disappeared into the bowels of the North Harvard Grammar School.

My life assumed a pattern. I was going to school. My teacher's name was Miss Travis. Every morning brought pleasant surprises; new boys and girls to meet, new lessons to study, errands to run, a quota of play to consummate, a given number of meals to be eaten—and suddenly, when my back was turned, night would fall and, exhausted, I would be chased, or carried off, to bed.

I knew that James Henry Sullivan was my father; I didn't remember my mother at all. Even when I tried I couldn't remember what my mother looked like, what her voice sounded like, or anything at all about her. To me, it seemed that Aunt Lizzie had always been my mother. My father was a stranger. He was always in a hurry going off to work in the morning, and many nights he wouldn't be home for supper. When my father came home late we would hear him ascending the front stairs; he seemed to have an impediment in his tread. When my brother and I went out to greet him we noticed that his breath was dominated by a potent element with which we were not familiar. As my Aunt Lizzie would start to warm up the cold supper dishes we would hear her say, "Henry's been drinking again." Everybody called my father Henry.

My father was a bookbinder by trade, as were all of his brothers. In those days, many young Cambridge boys and girls who had to go to work at an early age went into the Riverside Press or one of the other binderies in that section. My father went all through life binding books and trying to make both ends meet. He was good at binding books. In appearance, he was thin and rather artistic-looking, with brown hair cut in a pompadour style, and his upper lip sporting a well-landscaped mustache. He dressed very simply. His one bid for ostentation was a heavy gold watch chain that hung across his vest, supporting a large elk's tooth. My father had a good sense of humor and enjoyed being the life of the party; when I grew older, people often told me how funny he was. At that time he didn't seem funny to me. He squandered most of his fun away from home. In the house, he was always serious. On several occasions I heard my aunts say it was after my mother died that he started to drink. When he was even mildly under the influence, if he heard the song "Love Me and the World Is Mine," my father would start to cry. My aunts used to say that the song reminded my father of Cecilia.

We lived, at that time, in a two-family house on Bayard Street. We lived upstairs and on the second floor there was a parlor, a dining room, two bedrooms, a kitchen, and a bath; in a sort of large attic right above this, there were four small bedrooms. Here, the ceilings slanted down with the roof. If you had to get up in the middle of the night, you had to get up in the middle of the room—or else.

The house was heated by a coal furnace, and lit by gas. Today, with the oil furnace, the thermostat, and electricity, light and heat are no problem, but circa 1900 things were different. The cellar had to be filled with coal to service the furnace, the furnace had to be adjusted and shaken down at certain hours of the day and night, ashes had to be sifted to salvage pieces of coal and coke that could be used again, and the ash barrels had to be filled and rolled out to the sidewalk to be emptied by the ashman. Then, for light, there were the gas jets and the kerosene lamps. Kerosene had to be transported from the grocery store; the grocer always tucked a small potato over the end of the spout on the can to keep the kerosene from joggling out on the way home. With the coming of the Welsbach mantle, lighting became an even greater problem. The mantle, placed over the gas jet, reduced the yellow glare to a soft white light; the only trouble was that replacing the mantle required a steady hand. The new mantle was set over the jet, and the gas was turned on and lighted. When the gauze of the mantle had burned off, the mantle itself was nothing but a fragile ash. A tiny zephyr or the slightest jarring of the hand would crumple the mantle completely. If you avoided both the zephyr and the jarring, the mantle ignited and light was available. In those days, I was new at it, but life to me seemed terribly complicated.

Aunt Lizzie dominated the household, and ruled her do-mestic domain with quiet efficiency. Not so many years before, shortly after her marriage, her husband Mike, who was a plumber by profession, had been stricken with lead poisoning.

This left him partly paralyzed and unable to work. To support herself, and to provide a home for her crippled husband, Aunt Lizzie kept house for her two sisters, Jane and Mary, and for her brother, Joe. It was a sort of community project in which the boarders paid five dollars a week apiece. This princely sum entitled them to a breakfast, a lunch to be packed and taken to work, and a big supper at night. Washing, ironing, and housework were included, and Aunt Lizzie paid the rent. The money she had left was hers to keep. Aunt Lizzie had her hands full, and not with money.

When my father joined the household, he was working for the Boston Public Library Bindery at an annual salary of $1000. When you divided this by fifty-two weeks, you learned that my father's take-home pay—if he was going home on payday—was $19.23 a week. From this sum he paid Aunt Lizzie eight dollars a week for the three of us. It was a tribute to Aunt Lizzie's skill that we all survived. There was always good wholesome food available. She baked her own bread, and on Saturday nights she made her own baked beans and brown bread. She would start off with a leg of lamb for Sunday dinner, and then, on successive days, there would be lamb chops, cold lamb, shepherd's pie, lamb stew, and finally the lamb bone was turned over to some neighbor who was operating a dog. My Aunt Lizzie never heard of Fanny Farmer, but she could make nourishing dishes by using only a few scraps and the punctuation from one of Fanny's recipes.

As I grew older I could never understand why my Aunt Lizzie took in my father, my brother, and me to further augment her cluttered existence. I felt that she should have turned my father away from her door and thrown his progeny at him. But this never would have occurred to Aunt Lizzie. She was born generous and charitable and had her own simple philosophy. She had implicit faith in the Lord and that He would provide. Aunt Lizzie never let the Lord down, and until the day she died it was vice versa . . .

During the week, from Monday to Saturday, we didn't see much of my father. He left the house early in the morning and would return from work at different hours in various states of exhilaration or depression. Our back yard ran into the back yard of a family named Dupee. The Dupees kept an enormous St. Bernard dog tied up in their yard. The St. Bernard never bothered anybody; he was content to lie around and doze off to dream about his younger days when, wearing his brandy lavaliere, he patrolled the snowy wastes of the Alps, burrowing into drifts to rescue lost monks and upended skiers. Some nights, when supper was finished and my father hadn't come home, I would help my Aunt Lizzie with the dishes. The window at our kitchen sink overlooked the back yard, and as dusk fell on a routine evening the yard was quiet and serene. However, there were nights when we'd hear a crashing through the underbrush; the Dupees' St. Bernard would then start baying and tugging at his chain, and in rebuttal we'd hear a human voice mumbling an assortment of oaths to augment the din. My Aunt Lizzie would raise her head from her soapy chore and say, "Your father is taking the short cut again tonight." After Mr. Dupee had shouted out of a window to restore his St. Bernard's confidence, and my father had emerged through a hole in the chicken-wire fence and made our back door safely, my Aunt Lizzie and I returned to the dishes, and all was quiet again.

Downstairs in our house there lived a family named Johnson. Mr. Johnson drove a hansom cab, and at night he met all trains coming from Boston at the Allston station. When my father left the city very late, he would take the train. If Mr. Johnson saw my father quitting the train in a variety of directions, he would assist him into the hansom cab, close the double-breasted doors in front, mount his high seat in the rear, brandish his whip, and drive off to deliver Father to our front door. Some nights I didn't have to be psychic to sense that my father and Mr. Johnson had made a few stops on the way. The hansom would come clopping up Bayard Street with Mr. Johnson shouting encouragement to his horse and my father rendering a madrigal from a relaxed position inside the cab. One night, things were so hectic in and atop the hansom as it turned the corner of our street it seemed the horse was the only one in the party who was sober. Suddenly Mr. Johnson seemed to master his vision, our house took dimension, he pulled the reins sharply, and the horse reared back; Mr. Johnson shouting, "Whoa!" tumbled back off his seat, clavicle over fritter, and lay inert in the street. I don't know who helped my father into the house that night. It might have been the horse.

These were the weekdays; Sundays were different. Every Sunday my father had the same routine. After church and dinner at our house, he would take my brother and me to visit our grandfather and grandmother in Cambridge. Leaving our house in Allston, we would walk down North Harvard Street into Harvard Square, then through Harvard Yard—the closest I ever came to going to Harvard—out past the Fogg Museum, up Emmons Street to Emmons Place. My grandfather and grandmother Sullivan lived here, in the last house on the right. Each week my father and his four brothers visited their father and mother; each boy brought a pint of whiskey to the old folks. They spent the day quietly, discussing the news and playing "forty-fives," a game my grandmother liked to play while taking frequent pinches of snuff. The bottle was also passed around occasionally. My grandmother had open house on Sunday, and all of her sons were welcome to bring their friends to spend the day. These Sundays always came to an end with an early dinner, and as twilight set in, my brother and I knew that the time had come to prepare for our collective departure. We also knew that my father, having spent the day with his family and the bottle, would be a trifle loose-gaited on our way home. After the good-bys had been said, my brother and I would flank my father, and we'd start off. It was a long three-mile walk home, and if you had met the three of us along the road you would have seen a peculiar sight: we looked like two sardines guiding an unsteady Moby Dick into port. . . .

At home I took things for granted. My Aunt Lizzie seemed to do everything. Occasionally, my other aunts would bring us presents or take my brother and me to the beach or on a picnic, but in any emergency or in sickness I always turned to my Aunt Lizzie. When my tonsils had to come out, Aunt Lizzie took me to the hospital to stay overnight. Dr. Fitzgerald arrived and looped little wires over my tonsils and nipped them off. Many many years later, I learned that Dr. Fitzgerald had left both tonsil ends in my throat, and that they are still in there today. When my throat was healing I could have ice cream. I would lie in bed at home, waiting to hear the tinkle of the bells on the horse's harness that announced the presence of Bushway's Ice Cream wagon coming up the street. When I had a stomach-ache Aunt Lizzie would pack me into bed with a hot flatiron wrapped in heavy cloth. With Dr. Fitzgerald, hot irons, and Aunt Lizzie, I survived.

In an effort to augment Aunt Lizzie's income, my father hinted that a man who worked with him at the bindery was looking for a room out of the city. The man's name was Mr. Geyer. My father gave him an excellent character reference and said that Mr. Geyer would be no trouble, since he could share my father's room and bed. Apart from two meals, according to my father, the income provided by the new guest would be clear profit. Mr. Geyer subsequently arrived: a big-bellied Teutonic gentleman with a cardboard suitcase. He seemed to be agreeable and no trouble at all. However, it soon developed that Mr. Geyer was not perfect; he had two weaknesses. The first was that he consumed great quantities of beer when awake. The second was that he had no control of his kidneys when asleep. It soon became obvious that we were going to have to strap pontoons on my father or petition the Coast Guard to open a station in the room. The final straw was when Aunt Lizzie discovered that the new guest had ruined the feather mattress. He was asked to leave. Mr. Geyer, being a gentleman despite his organic shortcomings, hauled his acid presence out of our midst.

We lived on Bayard Street for over ten years. One rainy spring night as we were all eating supper, my Aunt Lizzie announced that she wanted everybody to come home early the following evening. She said that it was very important. I sensed something ominous. The next night my Aunt Jane, my Aunt Mary, my Uncle Mike, my Uncle Joe, my brother, and I all assembled in the living room. Aunt Lizzie opened the session tersely. She said, "Henry has something to say." My father rarely had anything to say. Something told me that if my father really had something to say, we were facing a crisis.

Apparently too embarrassed to face the others, my father hung his head and said what he had to say to the elk's tooth that lay dormant on his vest. He spoke slowly. Rigor mortis seemed to have set in on every sentence he uttered; each word appeared to lie in state on his lips before it tumbled out into space. When my father had finished, the little group sat staring at him, stunned. My father had informed us abruptly that he was going to remarry. He was also going to move out of the house and take his piano and his sewing machine with him. My Aunt Lizzie didn't mind losing the piano, but she did mention that she really needed the sewing machine. My father was adamant. Addressing my brother and me, he told us that we could either come with him and his new bride, whom neither of us had ever seen, or we could stay with Aunt Lizzie. My brother Bob decided to go with my father. Young as I was, I felt that I owed something to a wonderful woman who had been a mother to me for some twelve years. I said that I would stay with my Aunt Lizzie. I never regretted it.

television

Radio is like television, but with better pictures.
—Radio writer Phil Davis

A year before Allen's radio show, facing competition from the quiz program Stop the Music, *expired, the gossip columnist Ed Sulli-van started in television presenting vaudeville acts. Sullivan re-mained a resounding success on CBS-TV through the 1950s and 1960s, for a twenty-three-year run. That the frozen-faced, humor- impaired Sullivan was able to establish a fixed place in the new medium was particularly vexing to Allen who, having made triumphant transitions from vaudeville, to Broadway revues, to radio, was unable to pull off the feat one last time.*

♦ ♦ ♦

the reason why television is called a medium is because nothing on it is well done.

♦ ♦ ♦

imitation is the sincerest form of television.

♦ ♦ ♦

in the beginning television drove people out of the saloons into their homes. but now that people have sets in their homes television is driving them out of their homes and back into the saloons.

♦ ♦ ♦

television is a device that permits people who haven't anything to do to watch people who can't do anything.

♦ ♦ ♦

the t.v. critic, who wouldn't think of going to an automobile plant and selecting one car rolling off the assembly line to criticize, will isolate one of a comedian's shows at random, lash it to his typewriter and pelt it to death with snide nouns, verbs, pronouns, adjectives, adverbs, prepositions, and conjunctions.

♦ ♦ ♦

in the beginning god worked six days & created the earth. today 1 director, 1 scenic designer, 8 writers, 4 painters, 6 carpenters, 5 wardrobe women, 4 cameramen, 4 assistants, 2 floor managers . . . 10 actors, 6 electricians, 18 stagehands & 20 musicians work six days and create a mediocre television show.

♦ ♦ ♦

after a few recent shows, dogs have been dragging television sets out into the yard and burying them.

♦ ♦ ♦

i have a theory that if a giant plunger was placed on top of radio city and pressed down suddenly 90% of all television would go down the drain.

Allen and his fellow comedians sought one another's opinions of their work. Here's Allen's report to Groucho Marx.

october, 1950

groucho—

every sunday, after mass, we stop for breakfast at the stage delicatessen. at this hour, max, the proprietor, is host to a motley throng. horse players, bookmakers, cream soda lovers and sturgeon gourmets. how i, a gentile, get in there, i don't know. since the same characters meet every sunday there is a friendly atmosphere rampant that no airwick can subdue. when the lox is running good and the cream cheese is spreading easily those assembled between smacking their chops and wiping their greasy fingers on their vests, will discuss some subject that is currently engaging the general public.

yesterday the air conditioning was not functioning at the stage. there was a gamey flatulent essence dominating the room but the flanken was lean and spirits were high. talk turned to the . . . show. every tout, every bookie and every questionable customer present had seen the program.

eating was suspended. chicken fat was shaken from fingers to point them. novy was shredded from snags of teeth to make way for encomiums. the countermen stopped slicing to mingle their opinions with those of the chef who looked out of the kitchen door while keeping his eyes on an order of scrambled eggs and onions not too brown. a fat man put down a dr. brown celery tonic bottle and emitted an effervescent burp while he paid his tribute to the hour. a man sitting on a toilet bowl swung open the men's room door and added his kudo to the acclaim.

everybody in the delicatessen agreed that the . . . show had been great. this is a cross section that the surveys never reach. i bring you this report to let you know how the man in the street reacted . . .

i thought the show was excellent . . . over all portland and i agreed that it had taste, intelligent fun and stature. regards—

f.a.

My Library Routine

In this excerpt from Much Ado About Me, *Allen tells how he discovered books and performing.*

On May 31, 1908, I was fourteen; it was a memorable birthday. At breakfast that morning Aunt Lizzie told me that after school I was to put on my best blue suit and go into Boston to meet my father. My best suit was always a blue serge two-piece ensemble consisting of a Norfolk jacket, with pleats down the front and a belt around the waist that buttoned over the navel, and a pair of knickerbocker pants. Each year, the week before Easter, my Aunt Lizzie took my brother and me to the Jordan Marsh department store in Boston where we got our annual wardrobe. Our suits always cost five dollars each, and with the suits, we also received a fried-egg cap. We called them fried eggs because that is what they looked like. The fried egg sat very tight on top of the head. The blue serge in the cap was quite thin, and a phrenologist could have read a small boy's head without troubling him to take off his fried egg.

My Aunt Lizzie told me that I was to meet my father at Con Keefe's on Dartmouth Street. Con Keefe's was a popular alcoholic shrine, a cheer chapel with all the routine accouterments: the swinging doors, the five-cent beer, the free lunch, the starched bartenders, and the inevitable quota of frowzy thinkers draped along the bar. Riding in from Allston on the trolley car, I wondered why my father had summoned me.

True, it was my fourteenth birthday, but I had had thirteen other birthdays on which my father had never sent for me to meet him in town. Something was up and it was my curiosity.

[A]t Con Keefe's . . . [m]y father was waiting at the end of the bar with another man; each had a whiskey glass within easy reach. My father, after checking his watch and complimenting me on my punctuality, introduced me to the other man . . . a Mr. Billy Hempstead. Mr. Hempstead was an austere-looking man with a bulbous nose, a tall forehead that went over the top of his head, and over-all boiled complexion. If I had been old enough to attempt character reading, I would have judged Mr. Hempstead to be the custodian of a thirst and, as acting custodian, to be fulfilling his every obligation to his charge.

As my father talked, he kept lubricating his throat, taking little sips from his glass. He divulged that since I was now fourteen years of age I could now go to work. That was the law, my father said, and since it was the first law I had ever heard him mention, something told me he was going to see that it was enforced. . . .

My father continued to talk. I learned that, during the day, Mr. Hempstead worked at the book bindery with my father. At night, however, he worked at the Boston Public Library. Mr. Hempstead each night dropped in at Con Keefe's for a light supper with some liquid embellishments. Insulated against elements that might ruffle his complacency, Mr. Hempstead stepped gingerly out of Con Keefe's down Dartmouth Street to the library, where he changed from his street clothes into a blue uniform and became a police officer from 6 P.M. until when the library closed. Mr. Hempstead walked from room to room exuding authority and silently implying that readers had better keep order if they knew what was good for them. The library employed a number of small boys in minor capacities, and taking advantage of Mr. Hempstead's contacts, my father had arranged to have him drag me into the presence of the man who hired these small boys.

The minute my father explained my status and the reason I was the only one of my age in Con Keefe's, Mr. Hempstead was galvanized into action. He and my father drained their glasses, took some cloves to chew so that in case one breathed on the other he would not be suspected of drinking, and, calling the bartender's attention to their departure, pushed me ahead through the swinging doors and off towards the library. When we arrived at the employees' entrance, my father waited in the vestibule and Mr. Hempstead said that he would take me upstairs. Following Mr. Hempstead up an iron spiral staircase, I finally reached a room that appeared to be fraught with books and people. Girls were putting slips into round carrier pouches and popping the pouches into a pneumatic device that snapped shut; wire baskets containing books were coming down on an elevator arrangement from someplace upstairs; small boys were taking the books out of the baskets, checking the slips, and rushing off into the yonder. In a corner, obviously in control of this tome tumult, stood a dapper man. He took our entrance calmly; he seemed to be expecting Mr. Hempstead. After I was introduced to the dapper party, I could now number among my acquaintances Mr. Pierce Buckley. For my information, and to fill in a lull, Mr. Hempstead whispered that Mr. Buckley hired the boys who worked evenings. After inspecting me, and apparently evaluating my potential, Mr. Buckley told Mr. Hempstead that I would have to take a civil-service examination; if this hazard could be surmounted, Mr. Buckley would find a place for me. This seemed to conclude the business at hand. Mr. Buckley beamed and withdrew. Mr. Hempstead and I went back down the spiral staircase. My father was waiting, and a full report was turned over to him on the meeting with Mr. Buckley. Mr. Hempstead, having served his purpose, then left to don his policeman's uniform, and my father and I started home.

Some weeks later, after I had taken the examination, I was notified that I had passed. Then a card came, telling me to report to Mr. Buckley. The library, at that time, was open from 9 A.M. to 9 P.M. seven days a week. The day staff finished at 6 P.M., while the night employees worked the three remaining hours. To augment their incomes, many of the day workers stayed over and worked two or three nights a week, or all day Sunday. These day workers had the key positions when they were on at night. The small boys, all of whom were going to school, were used only as runners or stack boys. The runner was activated by a series of circumstances. The reader, entering the library to obtain a certain book, looked the book up in the catalogue room, then noted its number on a slip of paper. Also on this slip the reader put the number of his seat in Bates Hall, the large reading room where he could await the book. The slip was turned in at the desk, placed in one of the pneumatic carrier tubes, and dispatched to the proper stack. If the book was on the shelf, it was sent down in one of the wire baskets I had seen in Mr. Buckley's department. The runner was then given the book and told to deliver it to the reader at his seat in Bates Hall.

The stack boy had the better job. He sat up in his stack alone. He had a small table, lighted by a green-shaded bulb that hung from the ceiling; at his right was one of the pneumatic devices that delivered the pouches containing the book slips. During the night, if things were dull, the stack boy could do his homework or read. The arrival of a slip was announced by a rush of air and the plopping of the pouch in a padded receptacle. The boy put down his homework, opened the pouch, looked at the number on the slip, and disappeared down the dark, narrow corridor. If the book was not in, the slip was stamped "Out" and returned to the reader. Otherwise, the boy took the book, placed it in the wire basket, and sent it downstairs. The stack boy had one other chore, that of seeing to it that all books sent back to the stacks from the reading room were put back in their places before he left at 9 P.M.

When I reported to the dapper Mr. Buckley, I was told I was to be a runner, and that I was to work regularly, Tuesdays and Thursdays. Mr. Buckley told me that some nights boys were ill or didn't report for work, and if I wanted to take a chance, I could come in on any of my off nights and see if there was a job open. I did that quite often. It was sort of a contest. If there were two places to be filled, and five boys hoping to get them, Mr. Buckley would line up the applicants, look them up and down until he had built up the proper amount of suspense, and, then, with a dapper finger, he would point at the two lucky winners. The three losers would slink out into the night.

All summer I worked as a runner. The runner's qualification presented no problem for me. All I needed was a sense of direction and enough wind to last me through the night. There was no school, and I only had to work at night. During the day there was time to swim, play baseball, and participate in the seasonal antics that a fourteen-year-old boy is supposed to enjoy. That summer I ran in a junior marathon held as a feature of the church field day. As the starting gun was fired I saw my father standing in the crowd. As the race progressed and I ran through the neighborhood streets, trying to keep up with the pack of kids, it seemed to me that my father suddenly started coming out of every saloon we passed, shouting encouragement. While I was trying to figure out how my father was able to come out of a number of saloons in different sections, and virtually simultaneously, I lost the race. Later, I found out that my father knew the route the race was to travel, and he had been taking short cuts to the various saloons to be able to give me vocal encouragement en route. . . .

In September, all this changed. I continued to work at the library, but I began to go to high school, the Boston High School of Commerce . . . and . . . things were different. On Tuesday and Thursday nights I had to work at the library, and on these days my Aunt Lizzie had to pack two lunches for me. As a runner I couldn't do my homework during working hours. I was too busy running. After school, where I had eaten my first lunch, I would walk from Roxbury into Boston, to the library—a distance of about four miles. Sitting in one of the reading rooms, I would finish my homework; then, at five o'clock, I would go down to my locker on the employees' floor, eat my second lunch, wash, and be ready to assume my runner's role at six o'clock.

If I had gone through life as a runner, I would have died winded rather than rich. A runner was paid twenty cents an hour. Working three hours a night, I earned sixty cents. Working two nights, my weekly salary was $1.20. This, however, was not my take-home pay. I was now a city employee. I had to go into Boston every Saturday and report at the City Hall. There I signed the payroll at the paymaster's office and took possession of my $1.20 salary. The trolley fare each way was five cents; ten cents deducted from the $1.20 left me with $1.10 net. Some weeks, if I was fortunate enough to get an extra night or two, my income zoomed up to $1.80 or $2.40. . . .

My duplex lunches, afternoon homework sessions, night work, and my eternal walking from school to library to home must have overly diversified my interests. My scholastic record was never mentioned audibly either around the halls of Commerce or at home. I had no time to go out for sports, although during my last year I did play on the second basketball team representing our class.

The library still kept me busy. I got to know the Bates Hall tattered literati who were a constant annoyance to the runners. They were a set of old people. Nightly, in their threadbare dignity, they would arrive and order ten or fifteen books for the runner to carry to their seats. For hours these frustrated pedants, men and women, pored through the mound of books right up to closing time. Some were supposed to be doing research for books that would never be written. Others were sedate cranks or harmless demented specimens who had literary delusions.

To counteract these petty annoyances, the runner was eager to join in an occasional occupational prank. One of the department heads, a Mr. Chevalier, was reputed to speak and understand Chinese. Whenever a runner could find a Chinese loose in the library, looking for something, he immediately brought him to Mr. Chevalier's desk and stood by to await developments. The developments were two: one frustrated Mr. Chevalier, and one baffled Chinese.

Most library employees, toiling in a world of everlasting quiet, eventually assume the characteristics of the mouse and take on the small rodent's attitude towards life. They seem to shrink in size, acquire a frail look, walk with silent tread, convene in corners, and converse in whispers. In our library we did have one exception. He was a man named Mr. Forsythe. As Mr. Forsythe wafted zephyrlike from place to place, a small gust with a suit on, you knew that he was a library man. Something told you that Mr. Forsythe had gone through the best years of his working life without ever hearing or making a sound. One day Mr. Forsythe suddenly raised a gun to his head, pressed the trigger, and, following a loud report, left the library and his small circle of tranquil friends forever. . . .

On occasional weekday nights I functioned as a stack boy. These nights I enjoyed. If there was no work, I could roam around the stacks after I had finished my homework and browse through the books. On one browsing expedition I found a schoolbook. It looked familiar. After close inspection I found it was an English translation of a French storybook we were currently studying in the French class at school. I brought the translation to school. It was passed around, and suddenly, to the amazement of the French teacher, the entire class started to turn in perfect translations on the written homework. When we went onto a different French book to be translated, the French teacher was again amazed to discover that the class that had been progressing so well had suddenly lost its grasp of the language.

One night, going through the library shelves, I found a book that told about the origin and development of comedy. It explained that the early jesters were deformed people. Many of the kings had collections of bowlegged, knock-kneed, hump-backed, big-mouthed, cross-eyed or long-nosed specimens kept at the castle. Different jesters were called for different occasions. On a day when the king was depressed and felt in a knock-kneed mood, he would send for his knock-kneed jester. The knock-kneed jester would enter the court and walk around knocking his knees until the king was reduced to hysterics. Having concluded his grotesque performance, the jester would exit to the echo of the royal guffaw. The book traced the history of comedy from Vice (the comedy character in the religious plays that taunted the devil by hitting him over the head with bladders and slapstick) down through the ages. To me, all of this was new and very interesting.

It also gave me an idea for a classroom assignment. In the High School of Commerce, there was one course called the salesmanship course. Once a week, every student in this course had to prepare and deliver a five-minute talk on any subject he cared to select. The teacher of this course would often demonstrate the proper approach and technique. During the demonstration the teacher hinted that if the potential sales-man prefaced his sales talk with a funny story it would tend to relax the customer and soften his resistance.

Most of the talks by the students in this salesmanship course were pretty deadly. The subject matter, culled from the editorial columns, ran the gamut from "The Danger of Log Jams in Minnesota" to "Flora and Fauna Peculiar to Putney, Vermont." I remember that the title of one student's talk was "Should the Abolishment of Billboards Be Done Away With?" . . .

It seemed to me that a talk on comedy would be a little live-lier and a welcome change from the customary dreary recitals the teacher and class had to endure. Accordingly, with my recent reading in the library in mind, I prepared my talk. The class received the story of the kings and their deformed jesters very well, but the teacher lit into me in no uncertain terms the minute I sat down. He said that there was a time and place for everything: he added that the schoolroom was no place to dis-cuss comedy, and so forth. . . .

One night when I came home, my Aunt Lizzie gave me news of [a] change . . . we were going to . . . move to . . . Dorchester. . . . In this new neighborhood I had few friends; I was away so much at school and the library that at first I didn't have time to get to know the kids my own age. Left to my own devices, I started to learn how to juggle; I did this whenever I had an odd hour or two at home. Whatever pos-sessed me to want to learn how to juggle, I will never know. I taught myself how to juggle three tennis balls and three tin plates, and I practiced balancing feathers, broomsticks, and heavier objects on my chin and forehead. Whenever I saw a juggler I tried to duplicate his easier tricks. I was able to go to the theatre now because my income had improved. At the library I had been promoted: on Sundays I was now the assistant in the children's room. The head of the children's room on Sunday was a young man named Constance E. McGuire. Today he is an economist of great renown, but in 1910 he was a brilliant student attending Harvard on a scholarship and earning a few needed dollars tutoring and working in the library. "Connie," as we called him, was very helpful to me. After I had been his assistant for two years, and he was about to leave the library to study in Europe, he told the librarian that I knew the children's room better than anyone else on the Sunday staff. The result was that I became head of the children's room on Sundays. . . .

Every week I walked around and looked at the lobby photographs in every vaudeville theatre in Boston. When I found a picture of a juggler, I would manage to see his act during an afternoon after school, on my way to work at the library. If the juggler had an unusual trick or routine, I would study it and try to duplicate it when I got back home. My juggling was steadily improving. Moreover, I had heard one or two jugglers telling jokes, and now I started saving jokes that I thought were funny. . . . I continued to practice my juggling. I watched every new juggler who came to Boston and kept trying to master new tricks. The weeks flew by, and one day I received an unexpected invitation. The library employees were planning a show, with the talent to be supplied by the employees themselves. Some busybody had heard that I could do some juggling tricks, and I was invited to perform. I had been a library employee for over four years; I couldn't very well refuse. After

I had agreed to appear, I started to worry. I had never juggled in public, and as the date of the show grew closer I became panicky. I knew that I had to have some sort of an act. I arranged a routine of the various tricks I could do with the tennis balls, the plates, the cigar boxes, and the silk hats. I even memorized a few jokes ("I had a dream last night. I dreamed I was eating flannel cakes. When I woke up the blanket was half gone").

The eventful night arrived. As the show wore on, it became evident to those assembled that the talent of the library employees was limited to two types of endeavor. Every girl was a singer or a dancer. Every boy was vice versa. After an hour or so of amateur chanting and clogging I made my appearance with my juggling act and my attempt at comedy. I was a great success. When the show was over, I was surrounded by enthusiastic admirers. I stood there treading adulation for a time. As I started to pack up my cigar boxes and hats, a girl in the crowd said, "You're crazy to keep working here at the library. You ought to go on the stage."

I often wonder who that girl was. If she had only kept her mouth shut that night, today I might be the librarian of the Boston Public Library.

allen v. hollywood

Allen disdained Hollywood—the rigid pecking order, the prevalent fear, the monotonous pace of production, the relentlessly sunny days, the rampant phoniness.

Excerpts from two letters Allen wrote while making a picture.

hollywood
july 12th 1940

dear alton*

. . . the sun comes out daily and shines with monotonous regularity. i am getting to hate the sight of the solar ball and am considering asking the n.b.c. soundman over some day, with his equipment, to let a few claps of thunder and a rainstorm loose around the apartment. if the government wants to help the cotton growers i am submitting an idea that may be worth something. hundreds of easterners come here annually and after staying for a few weeks get homesick for the sight of a cloud. if the government will send cotton out here people can make portable clouds and keep them around the house. when a person gets a cloud-yen the cloud can be taken out of the closet and tacked to the ceiling until such a time as the visitor is resigned to return and face the eternal ultra-violet body suspended above by something einstein hasn't figured

---

*Alton Cook, TV, radio and movie critic of the *New York World Telegram*.

out yet . . . upon arriving i received some sage advice from an actor acquaintance. he told me to speak only to pale people. pale people are the ones who are working. the man with the deep bronze tan obviously spends his days in the open and consequently is inactive and prone to panhandle.

there's nothing in hollywood but optimism and oranges. destroy one or the other, you destroy the whole system.

the people here seem to live in a little world which shuts out the rest of the universe and everyone appears to be faking life. the actors and writers live in fear, and nothing, including the houses, seems permanent.

when an actor dies and is buried most of the agents have it in their contracts that they have the flower rights to the grave for ten years with options. by the time an actor gets ready to die he hasn't enough friends left out there to act as pallbearers. at most funerals the six men you see motivating the casket are from central casting.

darryl zanuck has so many yes-men following him around the studio i have often thought that he ought to put his hand out when he makes a sharp turn. someday, he will turn off and the mob will keep going on walking and continue out the gate at the other end of the lot. if they ever get off the lot several of them will have a difficult time getting back in.

◆ ◆ ◆

hollywood
july 11th 1940

dear allen*

life here is an eternal siesta . . . nothing has happened to alter my opinion of the place . . .

---

*H. Allen Smith, columnist and author.

i am working on a saroyan play for my own amazement. it concerns a mild fellow with a super-inferiority complex. he is born in hollywood. he lives in hollywood. he dies in hollywood. all through life he hates hollywood but his timorous nature forbids him to criticize or give vent to his true feelings about the place. two months after he is buried a little bush [has] grown up through the dried soil on his bare grave. the bush thrives and in the fall produces a colossal fruit . . . a single raspberry . . . the posthumous opinion the little man had of hollywood.

In the following essay from 1949, multiply the fictional movie's budget and projected gross by 25 and it resonates today.

A FABLE

Once upon a time, at Grauman's Maltese Temple in the ancient city of Hollywood, there was held a studio preview. Giant arc-lights swept the welkin so that even god might know that on this night the motion picture industry had labored and brought forth another epic. The immediate vicinity of the temple was fraught with yokel. The minions of the law, plying their truncheons, beat back the surge of shrieking bobbysox young and stampeded the smirking herd of older drabs who milled about in their baggy slacks and frowsy housedresses. In the grandstand, across the road from the main entrance, a howling rabble paid raucous tribute to the waving movie celebrities as they entered the temple. When the celebrities had entered the rabble cheered nonentities. When the no-bodies had entered the rabble established a new low in audible eulogy and cheered itself. In the lobby of the temple a town crier cried over a network, coast to coast, to inform those in distant parts of the land that Surprise Pictures, Inc., was previewing its latest $4,000,000 technicolor extravaganza *Zombie In The Outhouse.*

While pandemonium mounted in the byways, inside Grauman's Maltese Temple, surrounded by his liegemen, sat the ace producer of Surprise Pictures, Inc., the great Leopold Lumpit. Citizen Lumpit, a ready wit if given two weeks' notice, had coined his company's slogan "If it's a good picture—it's a surprise." The divinity that shaped Leopold Lumpit's end had done a brilliant job of landscaping. Twenty years a genius, his every cinematic venture had been crowned with success. The word "no" had yet to be uttered in his executive presence. Tonight, as he sat watching the first showing of his new celluloid charade *Zombie In The Outhouse,* life, as he was living it, seemed good to Leopold Lumpit.

The picture's final scene, a veritable crescendo of technicolor, which showed the zombie mating two rainbows, faded out. Mammoth letters filled the screen proclaiming this to be "A Leopold Lumpit Production." Before the temple tapers could be kindled, Leopold Lumpit bounced from his seat and, followed by his eternal swarm of lackeys, made for the door. Once in the road outside of the temple, producer Lumpit instantly became the nub of an admiring throng. Voices filled the night.

"*Zombi In The Outhouse* will gross 10 million, L.L.," boomed a paunchy patrician from the front office.

"You've done it again, L.L.," echoed a buxom script wench with thick bi-focals in her lorgnette.

"Those costumes you sketched for me will have Adrian tweezing his hair out," added the wardrobe designer.

"It's your hit, L.L.," loudly announced the director, "I just followed your instructions."

"Nine song hits," enthused the music writer, "I merely copied down the notes as you whistled them to me in your office."

"You'll get an Oscar for that photography, L.L.," chimed in the cameraman. "The first day on the set when you took the camera away from me and started shooting those closeups, I knew it had to be a sockeroo."

"Those sets you built with your own two hands, L.L.," piped up a tall plebeian in white overalls, "terrific!"

"Your technicolor, L.L.—the way you personally mixed those colors. That lavender sun sinking behind those magenta hills. The zombie with his topaz sword charging the nile green salamander on his old rose stallion, superb!"

Each studio artisan, whose name had appeared on the screen, vigorously denied his part in the contriving of the masterpiece and fought to bestow all credit on the man he proclaimed— "Jack of many trades and master of all"—Hollywood's greatest brain—producer Leopold Lumpit.

Leopold was not allergic to homage. Every producer knows that, next to picture making, flattery is the second largest industry in Hollywood. At all previews, when his vassals waxed hoarse and the volume of their acclaim diminished, Leopold would bolster the lull with a rave or two about his own ability and pat himself resoundingly on the back with both hands. For, be it known, Leopold Lumpit was not only Hollywood's greatest producer, he was double-jointed as well.

But tonight Leopold was not reacting as was his wont at previews. He appeared ill at ease—and for a reason. Through the din of his adulators' bibble-babble Leopold heard a small voice. It was his conscience. His conscience was making a suggestion. Nodding his head Leopold abruptly forced his way through the cordon of sycophants and hurried to the side of an emaciated little man who stood in the shadows of the great

Grauman's Maltese Temple. The little man was munching aspirin. (In the ancient city of Hollywood aspirin tablets were known as writers' caviar.) For this shrunken, insignificant and trembling mortal was a writer. He had written the screenplay of *Zombie In The Outhouse*. Leopold took the writer's arm and led him away from the eyes of the multitude.

"What do you want?" quaked the writer, as Leopold stopped by the side of the temple.

"My conscience bids me speak," whispered Leopold. "For 20 years at previews I have been taking the bows. You hear what they are saying again tonight. *Zombie In The Outhouse* is a hit. But I am only the producer. Without you I could have done nothing. You wrote the story. You deserve the credit."

The shock was too great for the writer. He slumped to the ground.

His body was found the next morning.

The producer was the last man seen with the writer. The evidence was circumstantial. The verdict was murder, and it came to pass that Leopold Lumpit, Hollywood's greatest producer, was sentenced to death on the gallows.

Moral: never say a kind word to a writer.

Allen appeared in six feature films: Thanks a Million; We're Not Married; Sally, Irene & Mary; Love Thy Neighbor; "The Ransom of Red Chief" *portion of* O. Henry's Full House; *and* It's in the Bag. *Though none of them displayed the full range of his wit, occasionally the Allen point of view managed to peep through—as in the narration he wrote and delivered over the opening sequence of* It's in the Bag.

FADE IN on TITLE CARD reading: "JACK H. SKIRBALL Presents"—with a jaunty MUSICAL fanfare.

DISSOLVE TO:

A second TITLE CARD reading "FRED ALLEN IN IT'S IN THE BAG!"—the MUSIC abruptly stops as we

DISSOLVE TO:

FRED ALLEN. He addresses the CAMERA.

FRED ALLEN

Ladies and gentlemen this is Fred Allen. I'd like to ask you a simple question. Why is it when you folks come into a theater like this to see a picture, before you can see the picture, you have to sit there and look at a list of names for twenty minutes? Now, for example, in this picture, the first name you see is . . .

Allen rolls his eyes heavenward as we

WIPE TO:

A third TITLE CARD with the name JACK BENNY near the top.

FRED ALLEN (v.o.)

Who needs Jack Benny, a little radio actor, in a picture like this?!

As Allen mentions some other names, they appear on the card, one by one.

FRED ALLEN (v.o.)

We have Don Ameche, an outstanding personality.
William Bendix, a three-fisted he-man.
Victor Moore, grandma's glamour boy.
And Rudy Vallee, fresh from Yale.

A dramatic MUSICAL sting as we

DISSOLVE TO:

The next TITLE CARD—a list of actors' names: BINNIE BARNES, ROBERT BENCHLEY, JERRY COLONA, JOHN CARRADINE, GLORIA POPE, WILLIAM TERRY, MINERVA PIOUS, DICKIE TYLER, SIDNEY TOLER, GEORGE CLEVELAND, JOHN MILJAN, and BEN WELDEN.

> FRED ALLEN (v.o.)
> On top of Benny you have to look at a long list of names like this. Who knows who these people are? Who cares? You can find names like these in any phone book.

Another MUSICAL sting as we DISSOLVE TO:

Another TITLE CARD, reading: "Screen treatment by LEWIS R. FOSTER and FRED ALLEN—Screenplay by JAY DRATLER and ALMA REVILLE [wife of Alfred Hitchcock (for lovers of arcana)]

> FRED ALLEN (v.o.)
> Screen treatment and screen play. These four people are now out of work. You'll see why in just a minute.

Another MUSICAL sting as we DISSOLVE TO:

Another TITLE CARD, reading: "We gratefully acknowledge the contribution of MORRIE RYSKIND to this photoplay."

> FRED ALLEN (v.o.)
> Ryskind's contribution. In one scene, the family is

eating dinner. Ryskind loaned us a half a pound of butter so the bread would look yellow in the close-ups.

Another MUSICAL sting, as we DISSOLVE TO:

Another TITLE CARD, listing "WALTER BATCHELOR Associate Producer" on top and "Production Designer LIONEL BANKS" and "Director of Photography RUS-SELL METTY, ASC" below.

> FRED ALLEN (v.o.)
> Look at that top name: Associate Producer. He's the only man in Hollywood who would associate with the producer.

The orchestra HUMS ominously—as we DISSOLVE TO:

Another TITLE CARD, listing: Musical Director CHARLES PREVIN, Music score composed by WERNER HEYMANN, Sound Recording WILLIAM LYNCH, Interior Decorator GEORGE S. SAWLEY, Film Editor WM. M. MORGAN, Ass't Director JACK SULLIVAN, Dialogue Director WM. R. ANDERSON and Production Manager ARTHUR SEITMAN.

> FRED ALLEN (v.o.)
> Get a load of this mob. They're all relatives of the pro-ducer. In Hollywood, all a producer produces is rela-tives.

MUSICAL sting as we DISSOLVE TO:

A TITLE CARD reading: Produced by JACK H. SKIR-BALL

FRED ALLEN (v.o.)

Here's Mr. Skirball's name again. He's in twice, you see . . .
(Philosophical)
Well, it's his picture.

A two-note MUSICAL bridge, as we DISSOLVE TO:

A final TITLE CARD reading: directed by RICHARD WALLACE.

FRED ALLEN (v.o.)

This is Mr. Skirball's father-in-law, another relative.

DISSOLVE TO:

Fred Allen again, talking to the CAMERA.

FRED ALLEN (v.o.)

That's what I mean. Why should you folks have to sit out there and look at all these names? You know, someday I'm gonna get my own relatives and produce my own picture.

And my picture will start with the story, like this:
(As if telling a fairy tale)
One night, last November, an eccentric millionaire sat in his den making out a new will . . .

As he speaks, we

FADE OUT

INT. TRUMBLE ESTATE—NIGHT

FADE IN on a SHEET OF PAPER, clearly marked "Last Will and Testament." . . . At the bottom of the page a man's hand signs the name "Frederick Trumble." A lawyer's name is also visible: "Jefferson T. Pike."

FRED ALLEN (v.o.)
The old man signing the will made his fortune with one invention. It's a soap that doesn't do anything. It doesn't bubble, lather, or foam. If you're lonesome while you're bathing, this soap just keeps you company in the tub.

FREDERICK TRUMBLE, a white-haired old man in a smoking jacket, sits at a desk in his posh mansion and finishes signing the will. His disapproving lawyer JEFFERSON T. PIKE hovers into view . . .

JEFFERSON T. PIKE
(Sniffily protesting)
But as your lawyer, Mr. Trumble—

TRUMBLE
I know what I'm doing, Mr. Pike. If I want to change my will I can change it.

Trumble TEARS UP the old will.

JEFFERSON T. PIKE
But suppose . . . suppose you don't find this grand-nephew? Who gets the money?

TRUMBLE
I'll find him!

JEFFERSON T. PIKE
Well, let's hope so.

Pike . . . heads out the door . . .

FRED ALLEN (v.o.)
You know, I like a commentary with a picture. You don't
have to watch the screen to know what's going on.

Trumble watches Pike exit, then collects the papers from his
desk, and crosses to a painting on the wall . . .

FRED ALLEN (v.o.)
Now, if you're reading a newspaper or a magazine, you
go right ahead. I'll let you know if anything happens.

Trumble moves the painting aside to reveal a wall safe.

FRED ALLEN (v.o.)
This is a moolah refrigerator. It's a device that keeps
cool cash cooler.

As Trumble opens the safe, a sinister figure appears silhou-
etted in a window. . . . From the wall safe, Trumble removes a
gigantic wad of cash, an envelope, and a photograph.

FRED ALLEN (v.o.)
I counted this currency to save you the trouble. It's
exactly three hundred thousand dollars. Now, if you
don't believe me, watch the picture the next show and
count it yourself.

Trumble looks at the photo. Inscribed on the back: "Frederick F. Trumble—Age Eight Months." He flips it over to reveal the picture: an eight-month-old-baby with the face of Fred Allen, bags under its eyes, etc.

Trumble closes the safe, replaces the painting, and crosses to a table. . . . Five identical antique chairs surround the table. Trumble inspects the undersides of the chairs, chooses one, and starts to stuff the money into the seat.

> FRED ALLEN (v.o.)
> Uh uh uh, you see, the old boy's ready for inflation. He thinks stuffing the chair with money will be cheaper than buying excelsior.

The sinister figure at the window hovers outside.

> FRED ALLEN (v.o.)
> Don't be frightened. That shadow behind the curtain is only the director's brother-in-law. You see, the director has to find a job for his wife's brother in every picture.

The figure slowly opens the window.

> FRED ALLEN (v.o.)
> Now, if he stays behind the curtain, he gets ten dollars a day. If he comes out, he gets five.

The figure points a gun through the window [and] FIRES. Trumble clutches his chest and staggers.

> FRED ALLEN (v.o.)
> Oh! They're using real bullets. Well, that's one way to get a relative off the payroll.

TOP: Back from Australia in 1917, Allen briefly used a dummy in his comedy act to send up ventriloquism, just as he sent up juggling. (BPL)
BOTTOM: Moving up from small-time to big-time vaudeville, Allen's attire, as well as his material, became more sophisticated. (BPL)

Song sheet from the Allen movie he dubbed "Sally, Irene and Lousy." Louise Hovick, later famous as the sophisticated stripper Gypsy Rose Lee, also inspired the musical *Gypsy*.

TOP: Fred clowns for the camera as he and Portland arrive in Hollywood in the late '30s, where he starred in films while simultaneously doing his radio show from the West Coast. (FH) BOTTOM: The abiding love between Fred and Portland, apparent in this photo, was equally palpable in their warm, amusing exchanges on the radio show. (FH)

Fred and the denizens of Allen's Alley (LEFT TO RIGHT): Allen, Kenny Delmar ("Senator Claghorn"), Minerva Pious ("Mrs. Pansy Nussbaum"), Peter Donald ("Ajax Cassidy"), and Parker Fennelly ("Titus Moody"). (BPL)

TOP: Fred and Bing Crosby, who preceded Frank Sinatra as America's most popular crooner, and who, like Sinatra, was one of Fred's many guests on his radio show. BOTTOM: When Allen appeared unannounced during a Jack Benny stage show to demand a refund of his admission fee, claiming the act was lacking, Benny was momentarily unable to continue. (BPL)

TOP: Allen was on *Time*'s cover in 1947, the same year as Dwight Eisenhower, Mahatma Gandhi, George Marshall, Princess (now Queen) Elizabeth, Charles DeGaulle and Jackie Robinson. (*Time*) BOTTOM: Allen's formal education ended with high school, but, as this staged photo suggests, he continued his quest for knowledge in the fields of literature and humor. (FH)

TOP: Allen's days and nights were consumed with preparing the script for his program. He regularly wrote and rewrote deep into the morning hours, damaging his health in the process. BOTTOM: During the '30s, the Allens summered in a modest rented cottage he called "Gull's Privy" in un-chic Old Orchard Beach, Maine. But even on vacation, work on the show never ceased. (FH)

TOP: Allen's relaxed demeanor on the weekly program belied the obsessiveness and perfectionism that characterized his relentless search for the consummate comedy script each week. BOTTOM: Among Allen's penciled comic notions: "victim of connubial ennui; mystery—body disappears in adv agency—find him at conference—dead no one knew difference; you're a feeb." (BPL)

Trumble collapses to the floor, dead. After a moment, the figure approaches and places the gun in Trumbull's lifeless hand.

FRED ALLEN (v.o.)

This is the plot stuff. You old moviegoers think you know what's going on. But this trick still fools the police. You'll see. The cops will think the old boy committed suicide. . . .

Letter to writer Hal Kanter

September 3
1955

dear mr. kanter—
i have been working as a
toreador down in mexico.
i have been doing very w
ell and have become quit
e popular with the fans
who attend the biggest b
ull rings.
recently, as i turned my
back to reach for my c
apella with which i inte
nded to dispatch the bul
l (el toro down here) he ho
oked me with his horn. i
ignored the bull's gestu
re, snapped my cape
lla and despatched him.
several americans who sa

w me accept the horn say
that i must come to holl
ywood and go into the ad
vertising game. if i can
take the horn, i can lau
gh off the finger.
what do you advise, amig
o?
adios, miguel pedro

Assorted anti-Hollywood zingers.
(See more in Speech at Friars Club Roast of Bob Hope, page 168.)

hollywood was started many years ago by a writer who went west with a cliché.

♦ ♦ ♦

hollywood is a place where people from iowa mistake each other for movie stars.

♦ ♦ ♦

my agent gets 10 per cent of everything i get except my blinding headaches.

♦ ♦ ♦

hollywood is a nice place to live if you happen to be an orange.

♦ ♦ ♦

to me [hollywood] looks like waterbury on a rainy sunday.

♦ ♦ ♦

having fun in hollywood is work.

◆ ◆ ◆

priest hollywood—stained glass windshield.

◆ ◆ ◆

success in hollywood is as fleeting as any fragment of a second.

◆ ◆ ◆

hollywood horse wearing dark glasses.

◆ ◆ ◆

novel western picture—indians win a battle.

◆ ◆ ◆

(in Hollywood) opportunity only knocks but once. the other knocking you hear around is in the trade papers.

◆ ◆ ◆

the lack of confidence in the movie industry is reflected in the architecture of the movie theatres. each theatre has thirty exits and only one entrance.

the world's worst juggler

In December 1913, the Australian theatre owner Ben Fuller, on his honeymoon in Chicago, saw and liked young monologist/juggler Fred James. Two months later the budding vaudevillian, on the cusp of twenty, set sail from San Francisco for a tour of Down Under. Here he writes of the first leg of the journey.

When [I] arrived at the pier, [I] found the S.S. *Sierra* being stormed by a gay throng. A band was playing on deck. Passengers on board were holding animated conversations with friends who were on the dock. Stewards were rushing on and off the boat with wraps and luggage as new passengers appeared. Young girls on the pier were throwing streamers at other young girls who were aboard. Confetti suddenly filled the air. . . . There were still fifteen minutes before sailing time. The tumult was accelerating. Last-minute flowers and packages were being delivered by frantic tradesmen and perspiring messengers, final words of advice and shouts of *"Bon voyage"* filled the air, and tears were shed. A puff of steam appeared from behind one of the funnels, quickly followed by a sharp blast; the time had come to go on board. Gathering up all my bundles and packages, I walked up the gangplank. Inquiring at the purser's desk, I found that my stateroom was in the second class. As I started down the stairs, the foghorn emitted a series of throaty blasts, and by the time I found my stateroom the boat had started to move. The band was playing "Auld Lang Syne"; the air echoed with hysterical laughter as the final streamers and handfuls of confetti were tossed. If [anyone] had . . . shout[ed] *"Bon voyage,"* all he would have seen of me would have been one frightened eye, gazing out of a small porthole in second class.

The S.S. *Sierra* was a ten thousand ton vessel. Today lifeboats bigger than the *Sierra* are found on the *Queen Mary* and other luxury liners. In rough weather the *Sierra* was tossed up and down in a blanket of spray as though she were being hazed as part of her initiation into some briny sorority. In an angry sea the *Sierra* resembled a female housefly caught in a fizzing Alka Seltzer. She was in the middle of everything, but had no control over the situation.

My stateroom was a form-fitting gullhole (on a ship a pigeonhole is a gullhole). As you squeezed into the room, on the right against the wall were two bunks, upper and lower. Jutting out between the bunks and the door there was a small sink, above which hung a tiny mirror and a rack that held a carafe of fresh water and two glasses. At the opposite end of the stateroom, for purposes of ventilation and lighting, there was a porthole. My ticket called for the lower bunk, but when the passenger who was to share the stateroom with me turned out to be an elderly gentleman, I insisted that he take my lower space. The old man remonstrated feebly, but I argued that I, being younger, was more agile and better equipped to bound up into the upper bunk. He consented.

I demonstrated my superior bounding ability on only one occasion. The first night out of San Francisco I bounded up into my upper quarters; for the next four days I just lay there, an inanimate lump—seasick. I not only couldn't keep any food down; my digestive apparatus got ahead of me: my stomach was rejecting meals I had hoped to eat the following week. My *mal de mer* didn't seem to bother my roommate. Oblivious to my moaning and retching, he slept soundly through the nights, left every morning for breakfast, and spent his entire days on deck. When he returned late in the evenings, he washed, quaffed a final drink of water from one glass, and filled the second glass with water into which he submerged his false teeth. The second glass was my glass. After the old man had gone to bed, if my throat was parched and I was dying for a glass of water, I could look down and see my glass laughing up at me. To quench my thirst I had to upend the carafe. (Later, the old man told me that he raised sheep in New Zealand and had made more than forty crossings to the States.)

The day before we arrived in Honolulu, I was able to crawl out of the bunk and creep up on deck. The second-class passengers were confined to a small area amidships. A few deck chairs were placed around the boat's two funnels. There was no room to play deck games of any sort, although this didn't matter since there were no games to play. One small group of passengers, huddled together near the rail, I took to be actors. I didn't know any of them. But since I hadn't eaten anything solid for four days, I must have had that half-starved look that people used to associate with the smalltime actor, for one of the huddled actors unhuddled himself, came over to me, and invited me to join the others.

I was instantly brought up to date with the ship's scuttlebutt. There were six acts going to Australia to play the Fuller Circuit. There was Madge Maitland, the Megaphone Lady; Madge was an abbreviated lady who sang in a booming voice through a large megaphone. There was Estelle Wordette and Company, presenting their own original playlet, *When the Cat's Away*. The company consisted of a middle-aged gentleman who smoked a potent pipe incessantly. There were the Flemings, two muscular young men who did an acrobatic act that consisted of Grecian posing and hand balancing. Also present were the Littlejohns, the Diamond Jugglers, a man and wife who wore costumes studded with rhinestones, appeared before a black velvet curtain covered with rhinestones, and juggled Indian clubs that were bedecked with rhinestones. And then there was Doranto, a rather serious-looking elderly man who made up as a Chinese and provoked discordant melodies from strange-looking Oriental instruments. Doranto billed himself as the "Human Xylophone." At the finish of his act he made good his billing by causing alleged melodies to emerge from his mouth as the result of spanking his false teeth with two short sticks while manipulating his orifice. I was the sixth on the program.

Honolulu, as the *Sierra*'s captain had hoped and the travel folder had promised, was there awaiting our arrival on the fifth day. As the boat crept into the harbor, a noisy school of natives swam out to greet us. After a hasty welcome in their native tongue, the natives got down to business in broken English, and demanded that the passengers throw money into the water. If the natives had known there were so many actors on board, they would have postponed their swim schedule for that day. A few first-class passengers tossed coins to watch the natives dive for them.

Pago Pago was a six-day trip from Honolulu. The seasick interlude had left me weak. I was better, but my stomach still felt as though it had slipped its mooring. One morning I fell asleep in a deck chair, and one side of my face was terribly sunburned. After it had blistered and peeled I looked like a portrait of myself done by a colorblind artist. The peeled side of my face had a covering of new rosy skin; the epidermis on the other side looked dirty. Traveling with us second class was a missionary, an exponent of some vague denomination, and with him was his daughter. The missionary was on his way to the Samoan Islands, where he planned to teach the natives what they were doing wrong. Meantime he was not averse to having an impromptu tussle with Satan on the way. His daughter was quite pleasant, but the missionary shunned his fellow passengers as if he had caught them throwing stones at a belfry. The first time the missionary saw my face with the two-toned effect he went into action. I was summoned to the captain's quarter, and when I arrived the ship's doctor was present. The captain told me that the missionary had reported that a leper, or a man with a serious social disease, was rampant in the second class. I explained my semiraw appearance. The doctor examined my face and corroborated my story. The captain apologized. There was nothing I could do to the missionary. I knew his daughter was sleeping with one of the acrobats, and I thought about suggesting a title for a future sermon: "Look Around, Brother: Sin as well as Charity Often Begins at Home." I didn't, though. I merely turned the other cheek— the one that hadn't been sunburned.

Pago Pago, an island in the Samoan group, was then an American coaling station. The arrival of the *Sierra* was an island event. The natives lined the dock, exhibiting their handicrafts to the passengers as they left the boat. . . . As Max Fleming, one of the acrobats, and I came down the gangplank, a kindly-looking old native, wearing a loincloth and a tattered white shirt that some tourist must have given him months before, rushed up to us muttering one word over and over again and pointing to the hills. The native walked along the dock with us, still repeating the same word. Finally, Max said, "I think the old guy is trying to say 'girls.'" At the word "girls" the native smiled and pointed to the hills. Max and I nodded, and answered, "Girls" together. The old man nodded back and said, "Flends?" Max decided that this meant friends, and the native wanted us to augment our party. We rounded up . . . other fellows from the ship. The old man looked us over approvingly, muttered his version of "girls" again, pointed to the hills, and started off down a dirt road.

After we had gone about a half mile, the old man stopped before a path that led up a hill. When we had all caught up to him, the old man started up the path with the seven of us tagging along, single file. We zigzagged up through the thick foliage for fifteen or twenty minutes until we came to a clearing in which we saw a cluster of crude huts. It was obviously a small village, but its inhabitants were not in sight. The old man led us to what appeared to be a meeting hut. A wooden floor covered the ground. A thatched roof shaded the floor from the sun, but the hut had no walls. Anyone in the hut could be seen by any natives in the vicinity. The old man motioned us to sit down. After he had arranged us all in a large circle, the old man beamed knowingly, muttered "Girls" again, and added four more words to, what up till now, had been his one-word vocabulary. The new words were "flifty cents" and "half clown." His "half-clown" rate was for patrons coming back from Australia with English money. We all handed over fifty cents apiece, the old man clinked the silver in his hands, smiled, muttered "Girls," and trotted out of the hut. In no time at all he was back again, followed by five big-breasted and Percheron-buttocked native women. The old man smiled all around, muttered "Girls" again, and then sat on the floor joining us. The "girls" lumbered into place. The old man started to pound the floor with both hands and to chant an eerie refrain; the "girls" began some primitive form of mambo. The elephantine gyrations of these village housewives, the slapping of their massive feet on the wooden floor, the perspiration cascading down their fatty parts, and their droning *a capella* to amplify the old man's bleating could arouse only one desire in a male: the desire to flee. But there was no escape. The provocative cavorting had to run its course. We were sitting there, cross-legged, watching these Swamp Rockettes for nearly an hour before the old man stopped bongoing the floor and dismissed the thundering ensemble. The "girls" giggled as they rumbled by us on their way out of the hut. The old man, still smiling, beckoned us to follow him as he started back down the path to the boat. On the way we were caught in a tropical rainstorm and got soaked to our collective skin. I am sure that if the missionary later ran afoul of the old man and his sinful racket, the old man's hut was closed, the native women were saved, and tourists walking down the gangplank at Pago Pago in later years were never accosted by the smiling jungle Minsky muttering "Girls."

Allen's Australian tour began with a booking in a Fuller Circuit theatre in Brisbane, where he saw his name on a poster:

Personally Booked in U.S.A. by Ben Fuller
Special Starring Engagement and
First Appearance of
FRED JAMES
The World's Worst Juggler

Fred traveled on this first leg with an Aussie actor, Frank Herberte, billed as "The Descriptive Vocalist," whose act featured him singing in front of slides that depicted the scene of his song as well as the lyrics, so the audience could sing along.

Frank took me to the Menzies Hotel, an old wooden building that looked as if it had been defying time and the elements for eons. Inside, the hotel seemed bare, as if at an auction and the only pieces of furniture left were those that had been ignored in the bidding. The Menzies also had outdoor rest-room facilities. As the guest checked in, he was taken to the rear of the hotel, and there he had the privy pointed out to him. As the Menzies guest entered his room, he was given instructions that explained the presence of a candle which, with a few matches, he found on his dresser. This was his emergency kit. If, in the middle of the night, the guest was summoned by a call from nature, he arose from his bed and felt around until he had located the matches. Lighting the candle, he hurried through the hall and down the stairs, holding the candle in one hand and shielding the flickering flame with the other. When he reached the back door and stepped nimbly out into the night, a playful gust of wind sometimes snuffed out his candle; when this happened, the guest found himself standing in a strange yard in total darkness. . . .

Since I was doing only one show a day, I had a great deal of time to myself. Back home, playing the smalltime and doing three or four shows daily, there was never time to do anything. In Brisbane, now that I was better, there was time to do every-thing, but there was nothing to do. After a short walk one morning I exhausted Brisbane's points of interest. With ample time at my disposal, I took up the hobby I had put down when I left the Boston Public Library: I started to read. I realized that I had a lot to learn about comedy. To study the methods two famous authors had used in developing characters and comedy situations, I started reading Dickens and Mark Twain. During the eleven months I worked in Australia and New Zealand, I spent my spare time reading. I went through Shake-speare, Artemus Ward, Bill Nye, Eli Perkins, Josh Billings and the world of all the current British and American humorists. All the English humor magazines were new to me. I discovered *Punch, Tit-bits, London Opinion, Answers,*

Pearson's Weekly, and the others. I bought every joke book I could find in the different cities and started a collection of jokes and stories that I thought were funny. When I had an original idea I wrote it down and filed it away.

As my collection grew, and as I knew more jokes, I was able to write new versions of old jokes to use in my act. I learned that any joke or story can be told in many forms. There is the old joke about the policeman who found the dead horse on Kosciusko Street. He took out his notebook to write his report. The policeman couldn't spell Kosciusko Street. He had to drag the horse over to Third Avenue. This same story is told about the businessman in the Western Union office about to send his partner a telegram to meet him in Schenectady. He sends his partner a wire to meet him in Troy. Or the mother who sends her little boy to school with a note saying that the boy has been absent because his sister has smallpox. The teacher is horrified. She calls up the mother and berates her for sending the little boy to school to contaminate other pupils. The mother explains that the sister really has pneumonia. She couldn't spell pneumonia, so she wrote smallpox. A final version deals with the boy who is sent to the store to charge a pound of tapioca. The grocer couldn't spell tapioca. He sent the boy home with a pound of rice.

This interest in jokes and comedy led to my first desire to write. My early efforts were crude. My High School of Commerce education hadn't prepared me to weld nouns and verbs together in acceptable literary patterns. I have always had a great respect for writers, and even today I stand in awe of the person who can clothe his thoughts in words. Before I left Brisbane I resolved that, with the time I had to study as I played the Fuller Circuit, I would try to improve my act, my jokes, and my writing. . . .

On the road, playing the different towns and cities in

Australia, I lived at the pubs and digs patronized by the Australian acts. I enjoyed living where the Australian acts lived. After my candle experience during my dengue period in the Menzies Hotel back yard, I could step out into any strange yard at midnight with confidence, my candle aglow, face into a forty-mile gale and arrive at the privy as cool as an altar boy, my flame intact. After making successful appearances in back yards from Geelong to Dunedin, I did become a nocturnal cropper in Melbourne. During the Melbourne Cup season, I arrived to play a return engagement at the Bijou Theatre. The hotels and rooming houses were jammed. An Australian friend of mine took me to a house in one of the suburbs where the lady of the house had a room to rent in the attic. The room had no window; a glass skylight supplied both light and air. After the rent had been paid in advance, the lady gave me a key to the front door, and then took me through several rooms and down two flights of stairs to acquaint me with the topography of her back yard. My friend was waiting, and I guess I didn't pay too much attention. I rushed away and spent the entire day in Melbourne. When I came back at midnight, I located the house all right, and when I got inside I found my room in the attic. As I started to get undressed, nature nudged me. I lit my candle and started for the yard. I didn't remember anything about the interior of the house. Every room I opened possessed an occupant who was busy snoring. Everybody in the house was asleep. After I had tried every door without finding a room that led to the yard, I gave up and returned to the attic. Nature, however, had not given up hope; there was only one solution. Opening up the skylight, I placed a chair on a table and stepped out onto the roof. A short time later, I re-entered the skylight, returned the chair and table to their original positions, and went to bed. Down through the years I have carried the picture in my mind of some nameless Melbourne roofer sitting in a pub, repeating the story of the unusual bird that stopped one night on a roof in that suburb and was never heard of again. . . .

In the course of time, I got to know many of the smalltime Australian acts quite well. At first, they didn't look like actors to me. In America, you could tell the smalltimer and his wife two blocks away. The wife would be wearing too much make-up; she would be slinking along in some flashy ensemble, a ratty fur piece dripping off one shoulder; and she would be carrying a cheap oversized pocketbook of gaudy hue. The male smalltimer usually wore a derby hat cocked on one side of his head, a checkered suit, white socks, and low-cut patent-leather shoes. If he was doing well, the male sported a cane and wore a dirty-colored diamond horseshoe pin in his red tie. The Australian smalltime actor and his wife dressed like the average middle-class couple. They looked like any two people on their way to work, and the theatre was work to most of them. To be assured of steady work, the Australian smalltime comedian had to have four or five different acts, the dancers had to have a variety of routines, and a singer—like Frank Herberte—had to have a repertory that would enable him to change his act for many weeks. With the small salary, the little actor playing the Fuller Circuit could not afford to lose time in travel for which he was not paid. When he opened at a theatre, the little actor had to make good because he had to stay there for many weeks. On his small salary, the Australian actor could not afford to have original material written, and if he did have money, there were no local writers who could create songs, jokes, or scenes for him. To survive in their profession, most Australian performers had to resort to plagiarism.

The imported acts were their objectives. If an English or an American comedy man played the Tivoli theatres in Sydney, Melbourne, or Adelaide, the instant that act had left for home—and sometimes even before that—an Australian act would be doing its jokes and routines on the Fuller Circuit in other cities. Before I left for America, two Australian actors named Ship and Gaffney presented me with a cane. When I asked them why, Gaffney said, "It's a present. We like you. When you go back to America we're going to pinch your patter."

The boys happened to like me, and I received a cane. Most acts not only received nothing; they went back to England or America without even knowing that their acts had been stolen.

allen's aphorisms

Allen penciled random thoughts on the sheets of foolscap he kept in his pockets, some written as grist for his radio comedy, others for reasons known only to himself. Note how many of his lines carry a freshness, immediacy and universality that belie their advanced age.

Cautionary Admonitions

vanity is an underrated vice.

♦ ♦ ♦

if the people who cannot do anything would all go in a corner of the world and outdull each other, the creative people could get more work done.

♦ ♦ ♦

germans think with their bowels.

♦ ♦ ♦

during the samuel johnson days they had big men enjoying smalltalk. today we have small men enjoying big talk.

♦ ♦ ♦

our civilization is an organized injustice.

♦ ♦ ♦

most people knee deep in the little messes they call their lives cannot appreciate much of anything.

♦ ♦ ♦

a person should never own anything he can't get into a coffin.

♦ ♦ ♦

the best substitute for experience is being 16.

♦ ♦ ♦

man's emotions are stirred more quickly than his intelligence.

♦ ♦ ♦

important thing for man is to be—not to have.

♦ ♦ ♦

starvation, and not sin, is the parent of modern crime.

♦ ♦ ♦

if adam had been a chorus boy there'd be no human race.

♦ ♦ ♦

men do not fail—they give up trying.

♦ ♦ ♦

most of us spend the first six days of each week sowing our wild oats—then we go to church on sunday and pray for a crop failure.

♦ ♦ ♦

hanging is too good for a man who makes puns, he should be drawn and quoted.

Metaphors and Similes

everything in radio is as valuable as a butterfly's belch.

♦ ♦ ♦

as nervous as a jellyfish on a ford fender.

♦ ♦ ♦

the . . . coffee tasted like something you'd get if you milked a rubber reindeer.

♦ ♦ ♦

the appreciation of an audience is as short-lived as the life span of a butterfly who has died prematurely.

♦ ♦ ♦

busier than a pump handle during a temperance picnic.

♦ ♦ ♦

[the corridors at mrs. montfort's rooming house in manhattan] were so long and dark i had the feeling i was walking down a giraffe's throat. i had a room that was so small it had removable doorknobs. if you wanted to bend over you could remove the doorknob just in case.

♦ ♦ ♦

[trying to correct a typographical error] is like trying to sneak the dawn past a rooster.

♦ ♦ ♦

suit—looks like something a moth threw up.

♦ ♦ ♦

coffee so strong you could float a horse shoe in it.

♦ ♦ ♦

rain so scarce 300 jehovah's witnesses had to be baptized in the dust.

♦ ♦ ♦

his farm was so poor, the grasshoppers wouldn't stop there.

♦ ♦ ♦

[. . . a mountainous spinster who,] when she sat at her desk, looked as though she had just made a parachute landing and the parachute was all skin.

♦ ♦ ♦

it was so quiet you could hear a caterpillar backing into a globule of dew.

♦ ♦ ♦

as quiet as a mink moulting on a pile of peach fuzz.

♦ ♦ ♦

cool as presbyterian charity.

Felicitous Figures of Speech

peeling the onion of doubt.

♦ ♦ ♦

suffered [from] contusions [of] a former marriage.

♦ ♦ ♦

friendship ripened into apathy.

♦ ♦ ♦

won't say i hate you—but my admiration for you is under control.

♦ ♦ ♦

crows scared so badly by the scarecrow that they brought back corn they had stolen two years before.

♦ ♦ ♦

nature in a moment of majestic playfulness.

♦ ♦ ♦

a dull talk embroidered with platitudes.

♦ ♦ ♦

i rarely indulge in small vulgarities no matter how delightful.

♦ ♦ ♦

man is nothing but live dirt.

♦ ♦ ♦

owed landlady so much money she ran out on him.

♦ ♦ ♦

society for prevention of mediocrity.

♦ ♦ ♦

it was so hot i wanted to take off my skin and sit around in my bones.

On America

things might have happened change course of history this country:

> ink forgotten signing dec - independence
> horse not there p. revere went to barn

♦ ♦ ♦

fraudulence has become a national virtue.

♦ ♦ ♦

about ten percent of the people in america are trying to do something and the ninety percent are either ballyhooing, picketing, or condemning the minorities activities.

♦ ♦ ♦

from the looks of things, america is a cinderella playground and eventually it will be twelve o'clock and everything will turn into a pumpkin—which will be a form of farm relief.

♦ ♦ ♦

income tax dept.—what makes uncle sammy run.

♦ ♦ ♦

a nation of people thinking humdrum thoughts and doing unimportant things.

♦ ♦ ♦

we go by majority rule. if the majority was insane the sane would be in asylums.

Random Whimsy

proctologist's crest—finger rampant on a field of rectums.

♦ ♦ ♦

i had a hole in my pocket. some guy put his hand in the hole and stole my shorts.

♦ ♦ ♦

western card game—raisin bread for cards. winner ate 4 raisins out of a five spot to make ace.

♦ ♦ ♦

collection of early american bagels.

♦ ♦ ♦

[song title] those aren't spots on the sugar, mother—you're putting your dice in your tea.

♦ ♦ ♦

athlete won four letters—couldn't read sweater.

♦ ♦ ♦

octopus pitching—threw 4 balls same time—3 balls & 1 strike.

♦ ♦ ♦

old actress—saves dressing room doors with stars on them.

♦ ♦ ♦

fine spun dogmas.

♦ ♦ ♦

champion bed-wetter of wisconsin.

♦ ♦ ♦

carry corkscrew on boat never can tell pick up bottle with message in it.

♦ ♦ ♦

scare moths—came back darn holes.

♦ ♦ ♦

bit—man expense accounts—boss comes—have eat up to bills.

Philosophy

the world is a grindstone, and life is your nose.

♦ ♦ ♦

how to develop new power. every mon–wed & fri do something you don't want to do. tues–thurs & sat don't do something you want to do. sun—do as you please.

♦ ♦ ♦

the emotional world sees men and things otherwise than as they really are, it makes a picture of the object of affection & loves this picture, not its real object.

♦ ♦ ♦

a child knows far better how to live than does an adult—he can still live in the fullness of spirit because he has not yet come under the domination of his ego—he fears no king, even the majesty of death does not faze him.

♦ ♦ ♦

science wastes so much time trying to split the atom. it would be better if the small nugget of sincerity that exists in our world was split so that there might be enough to go around.

♦ ♦ ♦

the world's sum of knowledge has been multiplied a thousandfold—what of its wisdom.

♦ ♦ ♦

the heart is that which makes a man eloquent.

♦ ♦ ♦

man's life is perpetual repression. that is the essence from the cradle to the grave.

♦ ♦ ♦

terror of society is the basis of morals. terror of god is the secret of religion.

♦ ♦ ♦

the worst trouble with the future is that it seems to get here much quicker than it used to.

♦ ♦ ♦

without the wisdom of the learned man—the illiterate man could not be governed.

♦ ♦ ♦

existence has been thrust on people unasked.

♦ ♦ ♦

we all long for change. yet we fight for security which is insurance against change.

♦ ♦ ♦

one of the best things you can give a child is a respect for words—for the truth that should be in them and for the power and beauty which they can be made to yield.

♦ ♦ ♦

silence is one of the lost arts.

♦ ♦ ♦

the average man has his back to the wall—but there isn't any wall.

♦ ♦ ♦

one of the signs of culture is your ability to extract pleasure
from objects or events to which the ignorant are indifferent.

♦ ♦ ♦

every man makes mistakes. his success depends on which
wears out first—his pencil or his eraser.

♦ ♦ ♦

4 principal impediments to wisdom are authority–habit–
prejudice–& fake conceit of wisdom.

♦ ♦ ♦

the next war will be between those who won't go and those
who try to make them go.

♦ ♦ ♦

all the human race demands of its members is that they be
born.

♦ ♦ ♦

hope is usually futile and remains unfulfilled but without it life
would be impossible.

♦ ♦ ♦

the ability to circumvent women and the capture of food form
the basis of masculine wisdom.

♦ ♦ ♦

if you don't want what you can't have you will always have
what you want.

Definitions

a conference is a gathering of important people who singly can do nothing but together can decide that nothing can be done.

♦ ♦ ♦

lawyer—a coward's weapon.

♦ ♦ ♦

celebrity—person who works hard his his whole life to become well known, then wears dark glasses to avoid being recognized.

♦ ♦ ♦

marriage is love that can't take a joke.

♦ ♦ ♦

insurance—a contract people sign agreeing to go through life poor so that they can die rich.

♦ ♦ ♦

moth—a closet butterfly.

♦ ♦ ♦

success—the cheese in the rat race of life.

♦ ♦ ♦

a piccolo is the smallest instrument a musician can play in public and still maintain his self-respect.

christmas

Allen wrote the following letter to T. J. Smith (nicknamed Captain Gregg for reasons unrevealed) of the Young & Rubicam Radio Department, producers of Allen's program. Mrs. McRorie was a censor for NBC who combed Allen's scripts for material she deemed offensive.

december 25th
1939

dear captain gregg . . .

it seems odd to address you as captain gregg after calling you fatso for four years at oxford. but you have won your spurs, captain gregg.

this is christmas day. to us, in radio, it is monday. about the studio we sense that it is not just an ordinary monday it is a monday apart from other mondays. the momentous event that occurred in bethlehem 1939 years ago plays no part in the strange pall that hovers over studio 3 in the rca building today. the feeling of "all is well" and "peace to men of good will" is not inspired as a result of the ghostly incantations of the little dominie who is not there. the aura of concord and tranquillity is present on this hallowed day because mrs. mcrorie, the pontius pilate or pilatess of the script world is absent.

today hells, damns, buggers and hermaphrodites romp in the scripts. today, radio comedians rant and rave to their heart's content. today no names are cleared and the patronymics of the great are bandied about with abandon approximating impunity. today, the little man has his fling.

we in radio this day are thankful for many things. we are thankful that the guest star's spot looks semi-entertaining. we are thankful that but two of the newsreel interviews have to be rewritten. we are thankful that the sketch looks as though it will play. we are thankful that we have this work. we are thankful that we are alone to be able to do the work we have to do.

we are thankful for the many presents we received and that brings us once again, to you, captain gregg. we are thankful for the gulliver coffee cups. we often have new england midgets as house guests. new englanders are used to having urine crockery placed under their beds at night. these jumbo cups will be known as the "double-duty" cups about our humble quarters. they will be used mornings for coffee and evenings for midget relief. we are thankful, too, for the colored cravat. it will look well on me as i journey forth to interview the seagull gelder or the other guest we contemplate for the coming week. we are indeed thankful to you captain gregg for your thoughtfulness and your generosity.

we trust that you enjoyed a dulcet christmas . . .

a confused new year, captain gregg.

sincerely . . .

trueman goodbody

In 1949 Allen and his wife, Portland Hoffa, sent this Christmas card.

The First Chain Letter

This chain of good cheer was started by a shepherd in Bethlehem and is going around the world for the 1949th year.

If you break this chain you will lose every friend you have.

Before December 25th copy this message—"A Merry Christmas and A Happy New Year"

—and send it to everyone you know.

An old maid who completed this chain suddenly received a proposal of marriage from a stout gentleman in a red suit who came down her chimney on Christmas Eve.

A department store Santa Claus who broke this chain was reported by a small boy and lost his job the same day.

Warning! Do not break this chain!

—You will have—

"A Merry Christmas and A Happy New Year"

Portland and Fred Allen

———

Another Christmas Card.

Christmas Budget Plan
Enroll Today!

——

On December 25th you will receive hundreds of wishes. Your friends and relatives will wish you a Merry Christmas—strangers will wish you a Happy New Year.

On December 25th you will be swamped with wishes. The remaining days of the year you will be ignored.

How would you like to have someone wish you a Merry March 23rd—or a Happy August 9th?

———

Read This Amazing Budget Plan!

———

You can distribute your wishes through the year.

Select any day and be wished a Merry or Happy day when you want it.

Here Is All You Have To Do!

———

Deposit all your New Year and Christmas wishes with us immediately! At your convenience notify us what date you have chosen—one wish will be withdrawn from your account and we will wish you, as of that date, a Merry or Happy Day.

———

To Help You Start Your Christmas Budget Plan
—we wish you—
Absolutely Free!
"One Merry Christmas
and
One Happy New Year"
Portland and Fred Allen

doctors

"doctor—middleman for cemetery"

Allen, afflicted with chronic high blood pressure (the cause of his death at sixty-two in 1956), became a medical autodidact and hypochondriac. In 1945 George "Doc" Rockwell, a colleague from his vaudeville days, invited him to go trout fishing at Maine's Kennebago Lake. Allen wrote back that he wasn't up to such an event due to his illness, adding: "I've been on a salt-free diet so long I can run my tongue over the bible and tell which page Lot's wife is on . . . my testicles look like two Guy Kibbee heads."

Excerpt from a letter to a friend.

. . . portland was abed for one week with an infected throat. we had several horse doctors in to see her but they couldn't diagnose the case unless she agreed to put on a harness and get down on all fours. this she refused to do and finally she found a tree surgeon who treated tourists as a side line during the summer. this gentleman prescribed a caterpillar spray and finally, mrs. a's bark responded and her throat slunk back into organic oblivion.

Letter to H. Allen Smith.

september
18th
1942

dear "friend of zero mostel's" . . .

this is the first chance i have had to get to the mail. we returned to the haunts of the "little flower" last week but an aunt passed away up home and my brother was in the hospital. i had to journey to boston to attend the funeral. when i saw the open grave it was a great temptation. peace at last. the end of everything. a chance to relax until resurrection day.

i have been having quite a time in recent weeks. when i returned from the clinic i reported to a medico here and started to take potassium treatment for high blood pressure. potassium is powerful and acts differently on systems. i don't think many doctors are too familiar with the drug and i doubt if the doctor who started me on the treatment had had any previous experience with it. i went along for seven weeks getting blood tests and varying the dosage. finally, my system became saturated and i broke out in a lavender rash, my nose closed up and my throat got as dry as a bedouin's instep. i didn't sleep for ten nights. the doctor became alarmed and i have spent the past two weeks trying to get the potassium out of my system. i have been drinking kalak water and have been taking capsules and appear to be shedding the drug at a rapid rate. i will be fortunate if the doctor can get me back to where i was with only the high blood pressure. my entire summer has been given over to medicine and i know now what a guinea pig goes through.

since i have been through the potassium siege my mind seems to falter. i don't know whether i am through as a personality, or not. perhaps you can get me on your air-warden staff. i look well in a helmet. i can't sleep. i spent the entire

summer in an eternal blackout at the beach. i can see in the
dark and have just about enough wind left to operate a small
whistle if the pea isn't too heavy.

f. allen

*The following speech delivered to the American Diabetes Associ-
ation half a century ago, proved to be prescient in light of the fact
that in October 1997, a presidential commission recommended a
"Bill of Rights" for patients.*

A Patient Prescribes for the Physician

I certainly appreciate this rash gesture the American
Diabetes Association is making. I am probably the only one at
the dinner who is not an authority on the ailment. The only
thing I know about diabetes is that I am fortunate enough not
to have it.

As a rule honors such as this one are bestowed upon men
who have made some outstanding contribution to medicine.
Frankly, I have made only one worthwhile contribution to the
medical profession. Down through the years I have paid all of
my doctors' bills promptly. This, perhaps, should entitle me to
some kind of an award.

At the moment, I realize that I am violating every rule of
medical etiquette. Here am I, a patient, talking to a group of
doctors and the doctors are listening. Usually, the patient, in
the presence of the doctor, is permitted to list his symptoms
and, when he has concluded, he is expected to listen. Before
a patient can ask a question (in rebuttal) he finds himself in
the doctor's outer office with his bill in his hand and a nurse
fluoroscoping his pockets. A patient talking back to a doctor
is like a flounder protesting its predicament at the Fulton
Fish market.

Recently, however, an unfrocked intern at a pet hospital hinted, as he was turning in his scalpel and his white shoes, that the status of the patient is in the process of changing—especially the patient who reads the daily newspapers. A doctor has been writing a series of articles that threatens to enable the subnormal patient to become his own doctor.

This doctor instructs the reader daily how he can cure hydrophobia, throbbing noises in the ears, abnormal hairiness and similar common ailments. When he gets around to explaining surgery, the newspaper reader will be able to remove his own appendix with a potato knife and a rear-view mirror.

In the past the patient was wholly dependent on his family doctor. When a baby was born, the first person it saw was the doctor. Years ago there was a subversive rumor rampant that babies were being brought by the stork. But even little children discredit it today. Recently, in one of the progressive schools during class, a small boy had his teacher locked in a closet. The teacher, not wanting to inhibit the small boy, spoke to him through the keyhole and suggested that if he was in the mood for homework he could prepare an "Essay on Mankind." The next morning the small boy brought in his essay. It read "I asked mummy where grandma came from and mummy said the stork brought her. I asked mummy where I came from and she said the stork brought me. There have been no natural births in our family for three generations."

This small boy is a medical problem. A distinguished medical leader remarked, "A small boy who questions the stork will grow up to be a patient who doubts his doctor." There is a reason why the patient has his doubts.

In later life, the patient receives so many requests from charitable organizations asking him to help stamp out the Number One and Number Two Killers, he has the impression that medicine depends upon survival of two things—money

and research. The money he can understand. The research con-
fuses him. He reads about doctors in busy laboratories around
the country watching mice smoking cigarettes, to learn if a
non-smoking mouse will live longer than a chain-smoking
mouse. He sees pictures of guinea pigs with hypertension
lying around on tiny hospital cots, having their diastoles
checked every hour, to learn if high blood pressure kills more
guinea pigs than medical science does. The patient hears about
hundreds of hamsters locked in cubicles with telephone bells
ringing in their ears incessantly. Notes are being made on the
hamsters' reactions to learn if the telephone will shorten
the life of a big executive if he lives like a hamster.

Research, actually, is way ahead of medicine. At this very
moment, in the laboratories of one pharmaceutical firm, there
are three known cures for which there are no diseases.

The patient cannot understand why research, money and
skill get all of the credit for the advance of medicine. He feels
that the one element on which the entire profession depends
never receives any recognition. In the patient's estimation
the very foundation of medicine is the patient himself. What
can the doctor do with his penicillin, his antibiotics and his
wonder drugs if the little man with the ailment is not available
to try them on?

The patient is powerless. The doctor is organized with his
American Medical Association, the A.M.A. The patient,
floundering around with his germ, or malady, is hopelessly
outnumbered. And that is why I am here tonight. It is to warn
you doctors that I am forming a patients' union to be called
"The American Patients Association," the A.P.A. When the
A.P.A. is organized we will demand better conditions for
the patient.

The first thing we will improve is doctors' waiting rooms.
These are usually drab alcoves that contain a set of nervous

patients huddled together—and a few copies of some old magazines, generally the *National Geographic*. While they wait the patients upset themselves by exchanging symptoms and attempting to diagnose each other. A patient with a kidney stone opens an old *National Geographic* and reads about the rock formations in Peru. This gives him an inferiority complex. Now he not only has a kidney condition, he needs a psychiatrist. A diabetic patient looking at the sporting pages of the *National Geographic* sees a picture of two football teams playing a new year's game at some bowl. The diabetic patient sees it is the sugar bowl and goes into shock. The atmosphere of the average doctor's waiting room is depressing.

The A.P.A. will demand that every waiting room be turned into a small night club with a television set, bartender and a floor show going on during the doctor's office hours. While the patient is awaiting his appointment he can enjoy himself. When the doctor is ready to see him the patient will be in a rollicking mood.

The A.P.A. will take up the prescription evil. Today, the doctor gives the patient a prescription. The patient wonders what medicine he has to take. When he gets out of the office he opens the prescription and looks at the writing but he can't understand a thing. Either the doctor writes badly or the prescription is in Latin. If it is in Latin—and the patient is a Harvard man—he has no trouble. If the doctor writes badly, the patient is confused, he's worried. The A.P.A. will demand that doctors write their prescriptions legibly and in words of one syllable. Then even the ignorant patient will know what concoction he is on his way to have filled.

We have some other constructive ideas—heated bedpans for hospitals in cold sections of the country, smaller pills for oboe players, with their tiny mouths, and X-ray pictures that can be framed if they come out well.

I am sure that medicine will advance, that the A.P.A. will cooperate with the A.M.A. And, as the doctor of the future, even as the doctor of the past, looks at his books at the end of the fiscal year, he will realize that things in medicine have not changed—"the patient still owes a lot to his doctor."

◆ ◆ ◆

chinese proverb—trust nature rather than a bad doctor.

◆ ◆ ◆

doctors say man is about to enjoy a life span of 100 years. scientists say the h bomb can wipe out man in a day. these days you don't know whether to plan for the century or live for the day.

◆ ◆ ◆

throat dr—hangs around firework displays—people say "ah" he says you ought have tonsils out.

◆ ◆ ◆

i was in such bad shape i would get winded if i ran a fever.

◆ ◆ ◆

mr. burton halpert's an old juggler who is now over seventy and doubled up with arthritis, which makes him over a hundred and forty.

◆ ◆ ◆

feel like $682,941—like a million dollars less tax.

environmental report

Under ordinary conditions, a single thought would not constitute an entire category. But the eight prophetic words following demand to be an exception.

should seen this place when god had it

life, growing old and dying

"you can't take it with you.
did you ever see a brink's truck at a wake?"

Among Allen's essentially whimsical jottings are some of hues darker than one expects from radio's funniest writer. Yet the humorist's touch remains evident. The first piece, from Much Ado About Me, *is Allen's recollection of a character from his boyhood.*

It was . . . in my grandmother's house that I attended my first wake, when my grandfather Sullivan died. The wake was an Irish institution. When a member of the family died, the body was laid out in the front room and floral offerings were draped all around. Chairs were borrowed, and the neighbors supplied extra cups and saucers so that there would be plenty of tea and coffee available for the womenfolk. Great mounds of tobacco were piled up on the kitchen table, surrounded by clay pipes which were called "T.D.'s." Also, there was plenty of whiskey for the male mourners. For the two days and nights the wake was in the progress the members of the immediate family rarely slept. When the neighbors called, they first went into the front room to pay their respects to the deceased; then the men would gather in the kitchen, fill their clay pipes from the mounds of tobacco, take their glasses of caper juice, and join the general conversation. The exploits and achievements of the departed were embellished, his sense of humor was extolled, and his loss to the community was overly evaluated. As the night wore on, the tobacco fumes cast a blue haze over the kitchen, glasses were filled and refilled, the talk changed to other subjects, stories were told, occasional laughter rang out, and a good time was had by the many good friends who had gathered to see the host off on his final journey. The women assembled in the dining room for tea and coffee and perhaps a snack. Memories, encomiums, and anecdotes involving the departed were exchanged and intermittent tears were shed. In every neighborhood there was a group of old women who thrived on wakes. They would descend on the house in their glory, sitting through the night swilling gallons of tea, stimulating the wailing and the small talk. In the morning they would join the family for the church services, and if there was room available in a carriage, the old crones would go along to the cemetery for the ride.

Not only the women loved funerals. On our street we had a retired old gentleman named Tom Carpenter. Every time Tom saw a funeral wreath on a door he thought nothing of bursting into the house and taking over. It didn't make any difference to Tom that the next of kin, or those who had assembled for the weeping, had no idea who he was. He would bustle around the stove, making tea and coffee, send out for food if it was needed, wash the dishes, and keep things humming in general. Tom would stay on for two days and nights with no sleep, happy at his chores. He would be the last one out of the house. After the body had been taken to the church and the crowd had gone, Tom's work was still not done: he would remain to give the room a few licks with the broom so that the family could return to a clean house. Every few weeks Tom would show up at our house to report to my aunt on his most recent ghoulish peccadillo. He would be exhausted, with long dark bags hanging under his eyes. "Mrs. Lovely," he would tell my aunt, "I don't know what they'd have done without me. The widow went to pieces. I had to make forty pots of coffee and God knows how many sandwiches." When my aunt asked him whose funeral it was, Tom would answer, "Gosh, I was so busy crying and working I didn't find out."

♦ ♦ ♦

we ought to make a note to remind us not to live too long.
i meet people . . . i haven't seen for twenty years and i don't even know them . . . their teeth are gone, their navels are hooked onto their vertebrae, their hands tremble, their eyes are squinting behind bifocals and they show only too well the ravages of time. most of the drinking men i know of yore are worse off than the others although they may have had more fun arriving at the paresis stage.

♦ ♦ ♦

life is a lull between the stork and the epitaph.

♦ ♦ ♦

you can never trust an old organ.

♦ ♦ ♦

an old man sits around confronted with the debris of his aspirations.

♦ ♦ ♦

if i could get my membership fee back, i'd resign from the human race.

♦ ♦ ♦

if a man tries to live on the fat of the land, he discovers that the fat accumulates in his arteries and hardens them.

♦ ♦ ♦

days roll off eternity's assembly line.

♦ ♦ ♦

i find myself winded after raising my hat to a lady acquaintance.

♦ ♦ ♦

i can't stand up straight and i am almost crooked enough to run for public office.

♦ ♦ ♦

life is an unprofitable episode that disturbs the otherwise blessed state of nonexistence.

♦ ♦ ♦

years are all right if you haven't lived through too many of them.

♦ ♦ ♦

if you have a house, it disintegrates. if you have money, it disintegrates. you just keep on struggling until finally they put you in a pine box.

♦ ♦ ♦

guts never wear out if they are in your head . . . it's only when you're silly enough to keep them in your stomach that they show signs of wear and tear.

♦ ♦ ♦

the older you get the more people you seem to know in the obituary pages. my aunt is 84 and has outlived almost two generations. she doesn't know anyone but god anymore.

♦ ♦ ♦

if you have that pooped feeling—find what's pooping you.

♦ ♦ ♦

i never look back. i just keep breathing. that's the secret of survival and my motto—just keep breathing.

♦ ♦ ♦

it is a pity we cannot escape from life when we are young.

♦ ♦ ♦

every old man walks with short steps. he wants to prolong the day which leads to its end in the grave.

♦ ♦ ♦

stand by for the big show. life is only the overture.

♦ ♦ ♦

life is futile and the man who wears a toupee should take off his hat to no one.

♦ ♦ ♦

life is a biological misadventure terminated on the shoulders of six strangers whose only objective is to make a hole in one with you.

♦ ♦ ♦

life is an annuity paid out to you a year at a time.

♦ ♦ ♦

life appears as a masquerade at which we don a disguise.

♦ ♦ ♦

life—a snarl of fantasia.

♦ ♦ ♦

getting born—cost 200—get buried 75—cheaper die than live.

♦ ♦ ♦

[life is] all in fun. paths of glory lead but to the grave. you will find, if you live long enough . . . that paths of ignominy, paths of profligacy, and paths of skullduggery lead to the same incision in terra firma.

♦ ♦ ♦

life is a theatre in which the worst people often have the best seats.

♦ ♦ ♦

i am not a small time confucius. i am not poor richard. i am merely a resident of dorchester doomed by some evil fairy around mosely street to roam the earth until such time as my penance has been paid.

♦ ♦ ♦

Finally, this line from Allen's early vaudeville years.

she was so old, when they lit the candles on her birthday cake, six people were overcome from the heat.

manhattan, the stock exchange, philadelphia, boston, gloucester, california, hartford, maine, montauk, new jersey, texas, florida and bermuda

How the subway has Manhattan commuters
so mixed up, you can't tell what part of
New York anyone comes from

A man who lives in Jackson Heights goes down into the subway with his lungs full of good, invigorating Long Island air. He rides downtown. Another man gets on at Canal Street. His lungs are filled with that good old bowery carbon monoxide. The two men are jammed together. They keep breathing in each other's faces. By the time they get downtown the Canal Street man's lungs are full of Long Island air and the other man is full of carbon monoxide. That is why, thanks to the subway, the people who live on Canal Street look better than people who live in Jackson Heights.

◆ ◆ ◆

the mayor has started a drive picking up delinquent girls on broadway at night. if this keeps up several sinatra fan clubs will be in jail shortly.

◆ ◆ ◆

everywhere outside new york city is bridgeport, connnecticut.

Response to a charge that a joke of his willfully maligned the stock exchange:

gentlemen: no malice was intended and i am sorry to have incurred the disfavor of the gentlemen. i have considered committing hari-kari on the two points recently gained by bethlehem steel.

◆ ◆ ◆

in philadelphia i stayed in a hotel room that was so small what i thought was a thread on the floor turned out to be the carpet . . . [it was so small] that even the mice were hump-backed.

This jibe, Allen wrote, "aroused some zealous local politician who was sleeping in the pork barrel. he stepped out of the barrel and took me to task in print. he claimed that I had spread propaganda to the effect that all philadelphia hotels had small rooms and that as a result of my roguery the republican party was canceling its plans to hold its convention in philadelphia that year. To appease this fulminating ward heeler, I had to reply to several editorials in philadelphia papers."

Here is Allen's reply to an editorial titled "Philadelphia Fights Back."

dr. editor,
    the remarks made on my program concerned a small theatrical hotel in phila. twenty-five years ago. no mention was made on my program and no aspersions cast on the many excellent hotels in phila. today. i know that the benjamin franklin hotel is so named because you can fly a kite in any room. i know that the rooms at the walton are so large the world's fair is stopping there when it goes on the road next fall. i know that the rooms at the belleview-stratford are so spacious that the army–navy game can be played in a closet. and i know that billy rose rehearsed his aquacade in a sink in one of . . . [the] mastadonic bathrooms at the warwick.

◆ ◆ ◆

why is it in new york you never meet a man who says i'm going to philadelphia? he always says, "i come from philadelphia."

◆ ◆ ◆

i have just returned from boston. it is the only thing to do if you find yourself up there.

◆ ◆ ◆

Q: Does every boy in Boston have to go to Harvard?
A: It isn't compulsory. If you know the right people you can get out of it.

◆ ◆ ◆

the smaller the theatre, in most cases, the less consideration the management had for the actor. in gloucester, massachusetts, there was a theatre that had no plumbing or facilities.

across from the stage entrance there was a coal and lumber yard with two gates. when the new vaudeville show arrived on its opening day, and one of the performers inquired for the men's room or the ladies' room, the stagehand opened the stage door and pointed to the coal and lumber yard with the two gates. the ladies entered through the left gate; the gentlemen used the right.

♦ ♦ ♦

california—have bottle of rain in a museum.

♦ ♦ ♦

leaving california is always construed as a gesture of effrontery by the chamber of commerce. the chamber stoutly maintains that california is god's country and they have the screwball assortment of religious sects out there to prove it.

♦ ♦ ♦

at the age of fifty everybody in california starts looking like an avocado.

♦ ♦ ♦

the only time a native californian will admit it's raining is when he steps out the front door and goes down for the third time.

♦ ♦ ♦

mines are a mystery to me. if you dig a hole in the ground up in maine you get water. if you dig a hole in the ground in penn-sylvania you get coal. if you dig in texas you get oil. if you dig a hole in the ground in california you get 20 guys standing around selling stock in a gold-mine.

♦ ♦ ♦

up in hartford, i hear they have so many insurance men one company up there has come out with a policy that insures you against insurance men.

At Old Orchard Beach, Maine, Allen and his wife summered in a cottage he dubbed "Gull's Privy."

the season opens officially when the first frankfurt has seen its shadow. there are so many canadians here, they're putting a british lion on the merry-go-round and laying off a hyena.

♦ ♦ ♦

by end of sept. people in maine all stand around in houses—can't sit down—sold all chairs for antiques.

♦ ♦ ♦

you could never stand [montauk]. you can not only hear a pin drop here; you can sense the rustle of the fabric of the sleeve as the person's arm is raised to drop the pin.

♦ ♦ ♦

[new] jersey founded by mosquitoes—[they] brought people in to have food.

♦ ♦ ♦

[the] mosquitoes in new jersey are so big, one of them stung a greyhound bus the other night and it swelled up so badly they couldn't get it into the lincoln tunnel.

♦ ♦ ♦

the holland tunnel was built so commuters can go to new jersey without being seen.

♦ ♦ ♦

one thing i could never understand about the empire state building. why is it hundreds of people will come over from jersey and pay a dollar to go up on the roof of the empire state building to look back at jersey again.

♦ ♦ ♦

texas is still the state abounding in opportunity. in one small texas town they found oil in a cemetery. 400 dead people became millionaires.

♦ ♦ ♦

without sun florida is nothing but a mecca for grapefruit and denizens of the swamp.

♦ ♦ ♦

in the symphony of life, bermuda is a three-bar rest.

politics

Though we know nothing of Allen's partisan political views—except that he disdained yahoos from across the spectrum—we can observe that he was Mencken-like in his disdain for elected officials.

a train bearing the illinois legislature to new orleans was stopped . . . by bandits last night. after relieving the bandits of their watches and jewelry, the excursionists proceeded on their journey with increased enthusiasm.

◆ ◆ ◆

never contradict a politician in the middle of a speech. let him keep going—he'll contradict himself.

◆ ◆ ◆

many a congressman who has been yelling himself hoarse in washington all winter arrives home, when congress adjourns, to find that his wife is the speaker of the house.

◆ ◆ ◆

there's an old saying. if all the politicians in the world were laid end to end they would still be lying.

◆ ◆ ◆

From the January 16, 1949, program.

ALLEN—Well, Portland, enough about surveys. I think I'll get a paper and survey the news.
("Allen Stroll" . . . Fade . . . Orchestra . . .)
(Street noises)
PORT—What does the paper say?
ALLEN—Here's an item. Now coaxial cable makes it possible to send television shows from New York to St. Louis. I wonder if this is going to have any effect on the life of the average person.
PORT—Why don't you ask some people as we're walking down Main Street?
ALLEN—Good idea. I'll try this man coming along with the possum-hide briefcase. Pardon me, Sir.
KENNY—Claghorn—ah say—Claghorn's the name, son! Senator Claghorn, that is!
ALLEN—Well, Senator.
KENNY—Don't hold me up, son! Ah'm in a swivet. I'm in charge of puttin' on little ole Harry's inauguration.
ALLEN—What happens at the inauguration, Senator?
KENNY—It's a spectacle, son. First there's a parade four miles long.
ALLEN—Who's in the parade?
KENNY—All the people who came to Washington lookin' for jobs.
ALLEN—What happens next?
KENNY—Right after he's sworn into office, Harry and a few friends leave.
ALLEN—For the White House?
KENNY—For the Treasury.
ALLEN—I saw the president's budget, Senator. He's asking for higher taxes.

KENNY—Harry's gotta raise taxes, son. He's fightin' inflation. Harry's gonna find out if anybody's hoardin' money.

ALLEN—How?

KENNY—All men's suits are gonna have cellophane pants pockets.

ALLEN—Cellophane pants pockets.

KENNY—If the tax man wants to see how much money you've got—he just raises your coat and walks around behind you.

ALLEN—But . . .

KENNY—If people don't spend fast enough the government's gonna put uranium in the money.

ALLEN—Uranium?

KENNY—If it ain't spent in 30 days the money explodes.

ALLEN—But . . .

KENNY—Son, Atomic money will start the biggest boom this country has ever known.

ALLEN—Well, look, Senator. What about this television expansion?

KENNY—Television don't mean nothin' to us Democrats.

ALLEN—No?

KENNY—But, Son, every Republican oughta buy a television set.

ALLEN—You mean, looking at his television set . . .

KENNY—It's the only way a Republican is ever gonna see Washington. So long, Son! So long, that is!

ALLEN—So long, Senator.

From the June 22, 1938, program.

ALLEN—Washington, D.C. New Deal officials plan to put 1,000 beavers on the Federal Payroll to provide $30,000 worth of range improvement and conservation work in Idaho. *Town Hall News* invited little-known politicians to explain reasons for the government's sudden decision to subsidize beavers. Presenting, then, that authority on wind and beavers, Congressman Trundle Scat. Mr. Scat.

HARRY—The workingman will have a beaver in every pot. Two beavers in every garage. Beavers to the right of us, beavers to the left of us, into the valley of beavers.

ALLEN—But how will these beavers lift America's morale?

HARRY—The beaver will give a dam for his country . . .

travel abroad

> Went to Europe—
> Where did you go?
> I couldn't see where we went. I broke my glasses on the boat.
> —*Penciled note from Allen's vaudeville years*

MOSTLY ABOUT AN AMERICAN

"An American in Paris" originally was a musical masterpiece composed by the late George Gershwin. Recently . . . "An American in Paris" has appeared as the title of an M.G.M. motion picture.

In Mr. Gershwin's stirring composition the instruments involved—the violins, the horns and the piccolos enjoy a melodic gambol. Throughout the film Gene Kelly, and the other members of the Screen Actors' Guild, revel in a Technicolor junket.

In music and in the movie all is tres gay. The "American in Paris" struts a mythical Champs Élysées swinging a harpoon, instead of a cane, for he is having a whale of a time.

But what about the average American? The little man with the travelers checks who is lured to Paris by a color picture of a flaming crepes suzette or a Folies Bergere poster. What happens to this "American in Paris?" A recent survey conducted on a sightseeing bus shows that his days are crammed with confusion and his nights fraught with havoc. The American is frustrated at every turn. The first hazard to which he is exposed is—

THE LANGUAGE

The American arrives in Paris with a few French phrases he has culled from a conversational guide or picked up from a friend who owns a beret. He speaks the sort of French that is readily understood by another American who, also, has just arrived in Paris. The minute, however, the American attempts to make linguistic contact with a native, verbal bedlam ensues. The Frenchman talks as though his sinus and verbs are red hot and he has to get the words out of his mouth before they blister his tongue. The American can never make himself understood, he can't get the proper intonation. The Frenchman talks through his nose and sounds as though he has a violin string up one nostril.

As the American gains confidence he will occasionally risk a cluster of French consonants and vowels in public. This often proves embarrassing. One American who had planned to buy a set of andirons found, when he left the antique shop, that he had bought two old ladies, one of whom was in poor condition. Another tourist speaking import French rattled off something to a waiter at Maxim's. When translated he found that he had said "Who is playing that trombone under my potato salad?"

As the American "ouis" and "mercis" his way in and out of shops and cafes he finds that to get what he wants he invariably has to point. The "American in Paris" finally learns that to speak French he doesn't require a tongue—all he needs is a finger.

When he has become resigned to his language dilemma the American finds that his next problem is—

MONEY

Accustomed to his green, sound dollar, when he changes his first travelers check, the American is panic-stricken. His pockets stuffed with those thin tissue paper francs he feels like a man going to a masquerade as a wastebasket. To the American, French money appears to be jumbo confetti or tissue paper with murals. French money serves a double purpose. If you don't want to spend it you can wrap something in it. "All the world's a stage" and France has the money to prove it. Unable to hurriedly determine the value of a franc in terms of dollars the American is completely bewildered in the presence of a French shopkeeper. He employs the technique he uses back home with the tax collector. He holds out all of his money, and the shopkeeper, like the tax collector, helps himself. After one joust the American knows why the French tradesman wears a long apron. The tradesman doesn't need trousers. He always has his hands in the Americans' pockets. No American is ever held up and robbed at night. The tradesmen get all of his money during the day. The American notices an odd thing about the small metal coins—a magnet will not pick them up but a Frenchman will. The "American in Paris" often looks forward to the day of his departure when he knows he can get his francs changed back into money.

When he has learned to speak well enough to spend his money the American finds that the next difficulty he encounters is—

THE FOOD

The two largest industries in Paris are shrugging and eating. The Frenchman shrugs—the American eats. Three million frogs legs are served in Paris daily. Nobody knows what becomes of the rest of the frogs. In all cafes fish or meats are served smothered in sauce or gravy. In Paris what is sauce for the goose is not sauce for the gander. The gander has his own sauce. Foods that aren't decked in a mantle of goo are served in a sheet of flame. For the first time the "American in Paris" enjoys eating food he can read by. He also sees many a near-sighted chef with a barbecued hand.

The streets of Paris are cluttered with sidewalk cafes. The Frenchman is generous. He likes to eat out of doors so the flies can have some. There are hundreds of cafes and every cafe has a wine cellar. In Paris there are so many rodent dipsomaniacs Alcoholics Anonymous may have to open a branch for mice. When the American is told that the specialty of the house is pressed duck he knows that the chef is also a tailor. When he sees the maitre d' walking around in his bare feet, the American knows that wine is made to order on the premises. If wine is requested the maitre d' selects a bunch of grapes and steps into a closet. A little muffled squishing is heard and in practically no time at all the maitre d' steps nimbly out of the closet with red feet brandishing a carafe of vin rouge. On occasion, when the American tastes wool in his wine he knows that winter has come and the maitre d' has been stomping on the grapes in his stocking feet. A proper French dish is the snail which is sort of an inner-door shrimp. As a chef gets older he prefers to cook snails. A snail is the only type of food a chef can overtake while he is sitting down.

The American who eats three meals a day in cafes often becomes a glutton. During sundry nightmares induced by too much rich food the American sees himself spending the rest of his life running a small business—renting stomachs to "Americans in Paris."

The final and greatest peril to be faced is—

THE TRAFFIC

The American is impressed by the number of churches in Paris. In Paris there is a church on every corner. It has been put there for a purpose. It enables the American to stop in and pray that he will be able to safely cross the street in traffic. Traffic in Paris cannot be described—words would have to be invented. It is a symphony of tumult rendered by taxis, cars and bicycles all striving to attain a crescendo of chaos. The French taxi driver is a frustrated pilot. He zooms through the streets cursing because he cannot get his cab going fast enough to take off. The private cars are shrunken coupes whose hunched-over occupants look like human snails who have been crossed with greyhounds. Scooting in and out of traffic are bicycles carrying optimists, both old and young, who think they are going to get home alive. Most French automobiles have no brakes. The driver keeps his foot on the gas and his hand on the horn. High over the montage of din, at intervals, the piping tone of the policeman's whistle is heard. Instead of the regulation pea in his whistle the Paris traffic cop uses a petit pois. The American cannot be too cautious. A street should be named for the Unknown Pedestrian who tries to cross in traffic called "Rue the Day."

♦ ♦ ♦

The following is adapted from a piece Allen wrote in Paris for Art Buchwald's Paris Herald-Tribune *column in 1955.*

THE ALLEN VACATION SERVICE

Before going into the travel business, my service did most of the things an executive wanted to do but didn't because of lack of time. If you didn't have time to exercise, we would have someone do the exercise for you. We would go to your cocktail parties and read books for you to improve your cultural level. We would go to concerts and be bored for you. On occasions we would send one of our men to your home to have dinner with your wife and play with the children. We would send someone over to the house to have a second cup of coffee at breakfast and read the newspaper.

People warned me that such a service would never work. But it's been successful beyond my wildest dreams. As you know with all the mergers going on now executives are really strapped for time. I know of one fellow who disappeared in Detroit for four years. His wife collected his life insurance and set up a university scholarship in his memory. You can imagine her embarrassment when he turned up recently after a merger as the chairman of a large automobile company.

He had been in conference for four years straight.

Our service has been so successful that we had to merge ourselves with a travel organization . . . executives are much too busy to take vacations so we will take the vacations for them.

Here is how it works. The executive comes to us and says he needs a European vacation as he's overworked, but he can't possibly get away. Would we have someone take the vacation for him. We ask him how he would like to go, by boat or by plane. Then we find out if he gets seasick. If he does our man will get seasick for him. We find out how much money he spends, if he's a big-tipper, or if he is—just a minute, here comes a client now. You can see for yourself how we operate.

A harried advertising executive walks nervously into [our] office. "I need a vacation very bad. . . ."

"We can take care of that. . . ."

"I want to go to Europe but I haven't got the time. Could you send someone for me?"

"We'd be delighted. What did you have in mind?"

"Well, I've never been in Europe before. I'd like you to send someone to Paris, the Riviera, Italy, Spain and maybe Switzerland."

"This might get expensive."

"I don't care. It's my vacation, isn't it?"

"Do you want us to take your wife?"

"Of course. I never go on a vacation without my wife. Send her along too."

"All right. Now tell us what would you argue about with your wife on a trip?"

"The same old stuff. Looking at French girls, eating too much, drinking too much. I would get sore when she spent money shopping, and when she complained about being tired when I wanted to get out at night."

"How many arguments would you expect on a trip like this?"

"Maybe 100 small ones and 20 large ones."

"I've got a good fellow for you. He's argued with some of the toughest wives in the United States. Should he win any of the arguments?"

"The less he wins," the executive said, "the easier it will be for both of us."

"Do you blister in the sun?"

"Yes I do. I like to lie in the sun, but I really suffer for it."

"There will be an extra charge for that. It's hard to find anyone who will blister and argue at the same time."

[I] asked the executive many questions, and [we] finally agreed to send [an] Allen Vacation man over in May with his wife.

"Will you see them off at the boat?"

"I'd like to, but I'm awfully busy with conferences right now. I was hoping . . ."

"Don't give it another thought. We'll send a man down to see them off in your place."

"I'm very grateful to you," the executive said. "You can't imagine what this vacation will do for me. I know I'll feel like a new man."

"A European vacation is the best thing in the world for you. You won't be sorry you let us take it for you."

[We] shook hands and the executive bounded out of the office shouting, "I can hardly wait for May."

correspondence

Allen spent a day each week writing letters. Uncensored, he was able to indulge in the free expression he was denied on his radio show. Herewith a small sampling: four demurrals, two notes to children of friends and a subscription renewal. Additional letters are sprinkled throughout other sections.

march 14th
1941

mr. john j. mccarthy fire department headquarters
municipal building
new york city

dear mr. mccarthy—

mr. kershaw, of the texas company, has spoken to me about your kind invitation to dampen the ardor of four thousand uniformed men, who will attend the holy name communion breakfast on april 20th, through subjecting said four thousand uniformed men to an outburst of oratorical pyrotechnics using my mouth as the rocket base.

unfortunately, my radio chores keep me going sixteen and more hours daily seven days per week. this flagrant violation of the existing labor laws not only keeps me in hot water with the wagner act officals but the many hours required for the preparation and presentation of the weekly radio program take up the slack in my days which might otherwise be devoted to writing and memorizing talks to forego appearances at the many festive events to which i am invited.

i realize that it would improve my social status to be found in good company for a change. i know that the mayor's speech would be an inspiration to me in my future work. i have heard that the combination breakfast at the astor is excellent. but, even these temptations on the one hand will not shorten my days nor lighten my labors on the other. i am sure that if you were out squirting a hose sixteen and eighteen hours a day you couldn't find time to operate a sideline that involved watering lawns.

sorry that i cannot attend but know that you will appreciate my position. you can get even. if i ever have a fire you can send your regrets. i will understand.

sincerely

fred allen

♦ ♦ ♦

Letter to a fan magazine requesting data on Allen's life.

Dear Alyce . . .

Judging from the numbers of Radio and Movie fan magazines rampant, on the news-stands today, I take it that the mythical "Average Reader" is mildly interested in the private life of his, or her, favorite ether or celluloid star.

Thanks to the activities of the high-powered press agent, no stone has been left unturned in the drive to lay bare the innermost secrets, hereditary taints, and present foibles of the person unfortunate enough to be in the Public Eye at the moment. When we consider the scores of publications, and the hundreds of activities printed, it is surprising that the actor, or actress, finds time to ply his, or her, art. If the artist involved is lousy . . . the word "art" doesn't go. It would seem that the day must be an endless succession of flashlights and grillings and the nights turned into a series of flights between night clubs to be on hand when the Master of Ceremonies "innerduces" the celebrities.

Portland and I have been talking it over and wondering if anybody would be interested in a couple of people who are minding their own business. We have been hanging around on the outskirts of fame, and popularity, in the Theatre and Radio for the past few years but we have been loathe to set the world on fire. One of the reasons we have put off kindling the Universe is because we don't feel that we have reached the age mentally where we can be trusted with matches.

I know, if we ever do become famous, our X-rays will be printed in the Fan Magazines and I suppose I'll have to mail out my wisdom teeth, which I have been saving and listing as assets in my Income Tax. . . . Our every move will be known to the Man in the Street and the intimate phases of our home life will be pool room chit chat. IF . . . we ever become famous.

Today, however, there is a world-wide lull in our fan interest. Who knows what we are doing Today? To enable you to scoop Radio Burp and Microphone hullabaloo, here is a detailed account of how we spend the time between sun-up and night lunch. This is news!

7 A.M. We're generally still asleep.

8 A.M. Subconsciously, we feel for the White Collar Man who, at this hour, is dusting off his desk. We feel for him . . . but he is never there.

9 A.M. The alarm goes off but it is generally next door so we seldom pay any attention to it.

10 A.M. Australian Opera Singer starts vocalizing upstairs. In Australia, it is 3 P.M. the next day and the opera singer has neglected to change his larynx to Daylight Saving Time. It's

our tough luck and after the third fugue we decide to get up. The customary ablutions follow and we are ready for the dawn of a new day.

10:15 A.M. Fifteen minutes of leapfrog which is fast replacing the Daily Dozen in the better bedrooms.

10:30 A.M. Portland retires to the kitchenette where she spends a good half-hour preparing a bad breakfast. This generally consists of half a watermelon, which is served with tiddley-wink chips. Watermelon tiddley-winks is a game we invented ourselves . . . the idea being to snap the seeds into a large bowl in the center of the table using the chip as a motive for the seeds to get about their business. The seeds are later dried and dropped, with a metallic clink, into the cups of doubtful blind men who are not flying the Blue Eagle. Following the watermelon, a single half grapefruit is served but neither of us touch it. Long experience has taught us that the "squirt is quicker than the eye." Rather than diminish our purchasing power, however, grapefruit is still served. We have Peter-Peter, not the pumpkin eater, but a set of unemployed Siamese Twins who come to the apartment each morning for the sole purpose of consuming the spurting citrus fruit. Twins invariably confuse a grapefruit. The juice takes aim but, in the general optical confusion it never fails to dash between Peter-Peter's head and spatter on the wall. The laughter that follows Peter-Peter's liquid victory always brings tears to our eyes so we might just as well eat the grapefruit in the first place. We have sworn our allegiance though and as long as there is a depression, and a grapefruit left, Peter-Peter is sure of his . . . or their . . . job or jobs. Breakfast is hurriedly concluded with eggs, toast, a phone call and coffee . . . in the order named.

11 A.M. Finds Portland busy mailing the breakfast dishes to a correspondence school for maids at Rutland, Vermont. The

maid, a Mrs. Pratt, studied housekeeping through the mail and sensing a possibility in postal scullery work, opened a mail chambermaid business that nets her a tidy income per annum. For a small fee, and postage, you can mail her your dirty dishes, carpets to be beaten, and waste baskets to be emptied. Several of Mrs. Pratt's clients even send her their unmade beds via express. The dishes are washed at the Rutland General Delivery window, where Mrs. Pratt brings her portable sink each morning. When they are dried, the dishes are mailed back to your return address which should be plainly marked on the package. Mrs. Pratt makes the beds at the American Express office and as soon as the second pillow is tapped into shape the bed is off to the client. So much for Mrs. Pratt.

12 noon. While I am busy answering the morning mail, Portland goes window shopping at a motorboat agency. As a rule there is only one motorboat in the window which simplifies her task and after a few "oh's" and "ah's" at the propellor and paint job she is on her way home.

1 P.M. Usually, Portland spends the entire afternoon hitting herself on the head with a croquet mallet so that she will be in the mood to give dumb answers should anyone ask her a question later in the day. I sit around with an old joke book trying to find funny things to say on the radio programs. When we tire of our separate pastimes, we reverse the activities. Portland takes the joke book and I pound myself on the head with the mallet. The time passes pleasantly but we are both happy to stop when it is time for dinner.

6 P.M. If we have been invited . . . we generally go out to dinner. If not, we both stay home for tasty Chiropodist's Buffet which consists of . . . pig's feet and pressed corn. After bicarbonate and swizzlestick have been served for dessert, we

are free for the evening. Sometimes I make up as Mr. Farley and Portland disguises herself as a little old lady who has lost a registered letter and we play Post Office. Other nights, we go around giving our autographs away to people who are convalescing or perhaps we'll spend the entire evening jumping in ambulances with bags of fruit for people who have accidents and can't depend on their friends to bring apples and bananas to the hospital. We eat the fruit in the ambulance which saves messing up the hospital ward later in the week. By midnight we are both tired out, as a result of this wholesome sport, and glad to get to bed and be tucked in by Peter-Peter. We have twin beds and with the Siamese twin chambermaids we are both tucked in simultaneously and are able to pop off to sleep without having to keep getting up to tuck one another in.

So you see, Alyce, our lives at the moment, are unlike the busy, glamorous, existences of most of the popular Hill Billies and successful Radio Singers you read so much about in your favorite Fan Magazine. Of course, if we ever get famous the world will want to know what we are doing every minute of the day. This may prove embarrassing reading so I would suggest that you read this and ignore us from now on.

Sincerely . . .

fred allen

◆ ◆ ◆

april
17th
1948

dear mr. marsh . . .

i am in receipt of your letter dated april 16th.

when a radio comedian wins an award it seems always to be

contingent upon the comedian performing some function in return.

i have won several awards that entailed taking costly adverts in obscure magazines.

one year, i was given a "peabody award." this involved engaging a taxidermist to stuff me into a dress suit, and writing a speech—which later i had to deliver to a group that looked like an insolvent rotary club that rented itself out to attend drab gatherings of this sort.

now—boston university has voted me "the american comedian of the year." to accept this honor you ask me to come to boston, with some forty musicians and actors, and broadcast, on sunday may 2nd, from the b.u. campus.

unfortunately, we cannot broadcast away from new york city. our orchestra plays the "prudential hour" earlier on sunday evening. our actors have commitments on other programs and cannot leave the city. our guest on may 2nd is bing crosby who is coming to new york for one day to appear with us.

i am afraid you will have to take back the award and give it to someone who is less involved than . . .

yours sincerely . . .

fred allen

♦ ♦ ♦

march 19th
1950

thomas e. congden—

i am sorry that i cannot accept the yale record award.

in this country today we have 5,000,000 unemployed. i am one of the 5,000,000.

if you give me an award how will the other 4,999,999 feel?

in addition to relief payments and unemployment insurance they, too, may want awards.

this could result in rioting on the yale campus, further jeopardise the economic structure of our democratic form of government and cause the marshall plan to backfire.

i never look a gift horse in the mouth but i am not averse to looking an organization in the motive.

what you propose in effect is to exchange the effort expended in the preparation of an alleged humorous speech of acceptance, a trip to new haven and sundry hours of my time for a covey of negative tributes, a brace of boolas and possibly a chorus of the whiffenpoof song.

had you thought of me when i was a practicing humorist, i might have reacted. now that i am unemployed my presence on your dais could only be construed as an affront in retrospect to ogden nash, s.j. perelman, henry morgan, and al capp—earlier recipients of the yale record awards.

sincerely—

fred allen

♦ ♦ ♦

Letter to the young son of Allen's friend, Arnold Rattray.

february
7th
1944

dear everett . . .

portland and i received your letter this morning. you didn't have to bother thanking us for the book. portland picked it out. she noticed a little space between two books on your father's bookshelves and she really bought the book to plug up that crevice. if you want to read the book before you used it for that purpose i am sure portland wouldn't mind. if you enjoy the book, too, i know she will be happy when i tell her.

i guess you are too busy poking around the barn, and trying to fly your kite in that high wind you get at east hampton, to bother much with your mail. you had better be careful with those old shells. you can't drive a nail very far into a shell and expect to be in the barn for long. if you have closed the barn door you may rise unexpectedly, hammer in hand, through the roof.

at the end of your letter you say, "i guess i will stop writing. i am coming to the bottom of the page." it is always best to stop a letter when you arrive at the bottom of a page. i know a boy who never stopped his letters in time. he would keep on writing past the bottom of the page and write down one leg of the table until he finished. then when he mailed his letter he had to saw a piece out of the table and cut off the leg of the table, too, and send it along in a large paper bag instead of an envelope. another time, this boy was writing on a desk. he didn't stop again but wrote down the front of the desk and along the floor for nearly two feet. when he mailed that letter he had to tear off the front of the desk and pry up two feet of the floor. this left a big hole in the floor. his father and mother both fell through the hole and since the boy lived on a house-boat and his father and mother couldn't swim the boy became an orphan. this is why it is always better to finish a letter when you come to the bottom of the page . . .

fred allen

♦ ♦ ♦

july
12
1950

dear editor—

you are the editor of The Cape Codder. i am a subscriber.

when a subscriber writes to an editor it is usually to complain about the paper's editorial policy, the small-sized print used in the help-wanted columns that is keeping nearsighted people, who are out of work and have no glasses, from finding jobs or to berate the editor for misspelling the name of the subscriber's wife in the news story that told how the subscriber's wife fell off a stool at a howard johnson stand and spilled 26 kinds of ice cream on her burlap ensemble.

my purpose in writing this letter is not to condemn. i have no desire to add another gray hair to your editorial cowlick. i merely want to dispatch a kind word to you and to your little gazette.

to me The Cape Codder is a friend who comes to my door each week bearing tidings from the cape. the affairs of the outside world find no place in its columns. The Cape Codder chronicles only the happenings on the cape and the gossip and matters of moment to its denizens.

what other weekly gives you news and items such as these? (i quote from recent issues)

"now is the time to protect pine trees from destructive turpentine bark beetles."

"albino woodchuck shot by frank hinkley in commaquid."

"the striped bass struck in at pochet beach, orleans, sunday."

"cranberry clinic to be held july 12 and july 18. cranberry growers will meet to discuss bog problems."

"mildewed sails can now be prevented easily and inexpensively."

what other journal gives its readers pieces comparable to "orchard twilight," "the june woods" and "campin' on the island" by somebody who signs himself l.r.j.—colorful memories of happy yesterdays and tributes to fauna, flora and secluded nooks and crannies discovered by l.r.j. in strolls about the cape?

what other paper comes out on thursday to enable you to finish its contents and have its pages ready to wrap up a fish on Friday? the answer is—no other paper.

until i subscribed to The Cape Codder i thought that a cranberry was a cherry with an acid condition. i thought that a seagull was a thyroid pigeon. i thought the mayor of cotuit was an oyster. today, thanks to The Cape Codder, I know why the pilgrim fathers, who had the entire continent available for their purposes, chose to land on cape cod.

enclosed please find check for another year's subscription. may you and The Cape Codder trudge along down through the years enjoying the success you merit for a job well done.

sincerely—

fred allen
the belmont
west harwich
massachusetts

catholics
(plus a report on purim)

Allen, christened John Florence Sullivan and properly baptized, was a charitable, faithful Catholic throughout his life. Once in a discussion about tough Boston neighborhoods, he convinced a priest that the one he grew up in was rougher than the one the priest's parish was in by telling the cleric: "When the boys in [my] part of town came into church and crossed themselves they were black and blue for a week."

On . . . Sundays . . . before we went to my grandmother's house, we went to St. Anthony's Church. After the masses the priests always stood outside the church, ostensibly to greet the parishioners, but I am sure they also had another motive. They were always pouncing on the parents of small boys. After some nondescript talk about the weather, the parents were made aware of the opportunities available for their small fry as either altar boys or choirboys. One Sunday, Father McNamara stopped my Aunt Lizzie when she had me in tow. A few Sundays later I was wearing a cassock and a surplice and posing as a choirboy. For years I told a joke about this experience: "The first Sunday I sang in the choir two hundred people changed their religion." It was not quite as bad as that. The congregation was protected; the choir boasted some twenty other raucous small vocalists who could easily smother my nasal soprano.

Shortly after my debut as a choirboy I made my first appearance as an actor. The church presented a Christmas pageant. I was cast as one of the Wise Men (I was then about seven) bringing gifts to the Christ child in the manger. Dressed in a toga my aunt had made which looked like a long mess jacket, I came on the stage, and I can still remember the first lines I ever spoke to an audience:

> Myrrh is mine—its bitter perfume
> Breathes a life of gathering gloom
> sorrow, sighing, bleeding, dying,
> Sealed in a stone-cold tomb.

I didn't stay up for the notices and consequently never learned the critics' reaction to my first performance.

♦ ♦ ♦

Joe White, early radio's "Silver Masked Tenor," wrote to Fred about a neighbor's cat that mangled a filet mignon during wartime meat rationing. Here's Allen's reply.

may
4th
1945

dear joe . . .

i don't know hickey's cat personally but it must be a protestant feline. a catholic cat would never go into an icebox and mutilate a steak in these times. a methodist or lutheran cat will do anything. a catholic cat has to go to confession and it knows what would happen if it told of maliciously entering a refrigerator and attacking a defenseless tenderloin. the priest would probably go back with the cat and look for what remained of the delicacy. a protestant cat has no qualms about theft for there is no penance involved and the cat can get away with murder if it doesn't recognize the commandments. obviously hickey's cat was intoxicated when it committed the misdemeanor and i am sure that if you will call hickey's attention to the depredations his puss is committing in the neighborhood he will either make good the loss of your steak or he will make his cat sign a pledge and insure the people who have steaks that no drunken cat will jeopardize the chief ingredient at a future dinner.

    regards
    fred allen

◆ ◆ ◆

. . . radio has about ceased to interest me. i received a letter from a priest over in brooklyn who claims that our program is slipping. i am going to write and remind him that priests lay plenty of eggs with those sermons and they are still using the "loaves and fishes" and "the sermon on the mount" routines. a comedian has to hustle around and get new routines occasionally. after i write the letter i expect to turn lutheran.

◆ ◆ ◆

father burke caught two hungry men, at st. augustine's, trying to scrape the dessert off of a painting of the last supper.

◆ ◆ ◆

laziest catholic—1st every year says grace in front of a & p. saves trouble saying it over each meal.

◆ ◆ ◆

near-sighted bishop who confirmed knob on altar rail.

◆ ◆ ◆

priest with a stained glass eye.

♦ ♦ ♦

old lady at customs—what's in this bottle—holy water from st. anne's. why this is whiskey! glory be! a miracle already.

♦ ♦ ♦

Portland, born half Jewish, converted to Allen's faith when they became engaged.

portland and i have been preparing for purim. portland is experimenting with a new seasonal delicacy, a combination hamantaschen and pizza. in the traditional hamantaschen along with the prune, poppy seed or chocolate nut fillings portland sprawls a few anchovies. adding the anchovies if you have some of the hamantaschen left over after purim you can flatten it out and make a small pizza or a large pizza depending on the amount of hamantaschen or the original size of the hamantaschen, you had remaining. in the purim spirit i took out my shofar and blew it around the house for a few hours to have my lip ready for passover. i play the only cool ram's horn in town and word must have gotten out. i had a call from steve allen. they opened the benny goodman picture at the capitol uptown and the national winter garden downtown. steve asked me to double for him. he was over in the capitol lobby blowing the clarinet and i was down in the national winter garden lobby holding a jam session with three other cool shofar cats.

speech at friars club roast of bob hope

Traditionally the barbs at the early Friars Club "Roasts" of show business celebrities featured language unfit for publication in a daily newspaper. But Allen, a much sought-after speaker, brought down the house without employing the vulgate.

I appear before you tonight ladies and gentlemen with mixed emotions. The Friars is a most unusual fraternal organization. Some weeks ago I was sitting at home trying to summon up enough will power to turn off the television. Dumont, of course, not NBC. The phone rang. It was Jesse Block asking me to speak at this dinner. At the very instant that Jesse, the head of the entertainment committee of the Friars, was asking me to do the Friars a favor The Abbot* was on television telling some jokes that belonged to me. The U.N. delegates can learn something from the Friars technique.

To me, most of these dinners are alike. Prominent people are invited to attend and, in exchange for a blueplate dinner, they are asked to make a few extravagant remarks about the guest of honor. For the guest of honor, the experience is akin to coming back to life in a mortuary, and overhearing somebody reading his flattering obituary notices.

---

*Milton Berle

Most big dinners start with the selection of the guest of honor. The Friars work differently. They are afraid to plan a dinner until they know that Georgie Jessel is available. If Georgie can make it—then the Friars send out to Hollywood for a guest. They have to send out to Hollywood—most of the New York Friars are out of work. How would it look to give a big dinner for the guest of honor who was unemployed. Mr. Jessel, of course, is banquet insurance. Lindy is now sending out a $4 dinner. As the dinner is delivered, Mr. Jessel says a few words in the hall at the open door. Mr. Jessel has delivered the eulogies over so many departed calories and is so eager to speak—when food is exposed—you never know—after you have finished your dinner—whether the next sound you hear is some abdominal disturbance or the voice of Mr. Jessel. Frankly, I was crazy to come here tonight. Not only is it Lent, but it's Friday and the main course is meat. Luckily I spoke to Bishop Sheen this afternoon and received a special dispensation. I happened to bump into the Bishop at an Aftra meeting. Bishop Sheen is doing so well in television that his sponsor, Admiral, is making a new TV set for the clergy. It has a stained glass tube.

I know it is customary for a speaker to applaud verbally for the talent and the virtues of the guest of honor. I am sure there is nothing any of us can say tonight about Mr. Hope that he has not already said about himself. The true Hope story has never been told until tonight. I have some items taken from the secret files of Ralph Edwards.

The guest of honor was born in London, a conventional male baby, after the turn of the century. The boy was christened Leslie Townes Hope. At the christening they used milk. It was an English family and they were saving the water for tea. There were seven boys in the Hope family. Rather a large family, judged by English standards. The British are so reserved

they seldom get close enough to breed. The race is perpetu-
ated by foreigners and through correspondence from the
Colonies. As a boy, little Leslie Hope was prematurely poor.
To get enough food, he carried a little bicycle pump to blow
his kippers up into bloaters. He used to see Winston Churchill
leave London and return with bags of money. When the boy
learned where Mr. Churchill was getting his money he told his
father. The father said, "I've been downhearted. I'll take my
family to America. There I can raise my Hopes."

Arriving in this country the Hope family went right to Fort
Knox. When they were turned down, little Leslie said, "Don't
worry, Pater, I will go to work here in America and some day
the Hope family will have its own Fort Knox."

Years later, I met Leslie in New York. I was living in a small
theatrical boarding house—Mrs. Montfort's on 40th Street—
room and board a dollar a day. The room was a crypt with a
transom on it. The board defies description. There was a
plaque in the dining room where Duncan Hines fell. The landlady never served a rump roast for sentimental reasons. Her
husband had died from one at Sing Sing. The hotel was so cold
the actors were only able to keep warm from the heartburn
they got from eating the food. The whole place was filthy. The
only thing you could ever see through a window was an eclipse.
The mice in the place had athletes feet.

The guests at Mrs. Montfort's were broken-down vaudeville actors—Broomstick Elliott—the Brice Brothers—Myer-
Marie, a half-man, half-woman.

My first meeting with Leslie Hope came by chance. I had
loaned my tuxedo to a sword swallower at the boarding house.
The sword swallower had been out of work for two years. The
first show he went on—wearing my tuxedo—he swallowed a
long sword. The audience applauded. The sword swallower

lost his head. He forgot to remove the sword. He took a bow and cut the whole seat out of my tuxedo pants.

Well, I was on my way to see the tailor's about my pants. A young man stopped me and asked me if I could direct him to the White Rats Club. He told me modestly, in a loud voice, that he was Bob Hope, the comedian and invited me to step into a doorway and see his act. I did, and I knew that Bob Hope was going to be a great success. It wasn't his personality or his act—but he was the first vaudeville actor to carry his own candy machine around the country. When he was working on the stage, his candy machine was working for him in the lobby.

About this time Mr. Hope started creating joke material. Some time ago Olsen and Johnson bought the entire protected material files of the N.V.A. There was a letter in the collection that said, "Dear Mr. Chesterfield, I would like to protect an ad-lib. At one show today, my partner exited and threw me a kiss. I said, 'What is that?' She said, 'I'm throwing you a kiss.' I ad-libbed, 'You lazy thing.' I would like to have this protected." The letter was signed, Bob Hope. That offer must have ex-hausted Mr. Hope creatively, for since that occasion he has been surrounded by a day and night shift of comedy writers.

Mr. Hope's story is as well known as the Fall of Hadacol. He started in vaudeville with a double act. He told jokes so fast his partner couldn't get her lines in. Mr. Hope immediately became a monologist. He went into Musical Comedy. He couldn't tolerate the intermissions—they forced him to get off stage between acts. Motion pictures have no intermissions— he could be on all the time. Mr. Hope saw the possibilities of Hollywood.

Hollywood, the cinema capital, was started many years ago by a writer who went west with a cliché.

Hollywood is where a star is a person who works all of his

life to become recognized—and then wears dark glasses so that nobody will know who he is.

Hollywood is where a man running a tea shop failed and had 600 candles left over. With the 600 candles he opened a church and cleaned up.

Hollywood is where the Bank of America has a Vice President who sits in an office with nothing but a giant cuspidor. If you are an independent producer and you are going to make a picture with spit—you have to see him.

Hollywood is where 20th Century Fox is using Marilyn Monroe until it can get Cinerama ready.

Hollywood is where Mr. Hope went into Radio and Motion Pictures and was catapulted to success. . . .

With the many things that have been said about the guest of honor tonight, I'm sure that this season, the grass will grow green from the Waldorf to New Rochelle. Summing up, a frank inventory of Mr. Hope's assets are hereby listed. Mr. Hope is a lover of the things he likes.

Money has never gone to Mr. Hope's head. Most of it has gone to the government. Mr. Hope's fame is assured. Westbrook Pegler recently spoke well of him. Mr. Hope has written two books which proves that his flair for the trite has been manifest on more than one occasion.

Charity begins at home—but for a man who is never home, he does more charity than any actor who ever lived.

And finally—Mr. Hope is as good as his word. As a little boy he promised his father that some day the Hope family would have its own Fort Knox. As Mr. Hope sits here tonight, basking in adulation and wallowing in affluence, he knows that that day has come to pass.

Thank you.

# of things literary

"cherchez le writer"

—From Allen's Notes

*The disciplined Allen wrote every day, often through the night,
to turn out his program. "i am," he claimed, "probably the only
writer in the world who has written more than he can lift." He kept
the 50 large black leather bound volumes of his radio scripts on his
bookshelves (which occupied 10 feet of space) beside a one-volume
copy of the collected works of William Shakespeare (which took up
a mere three-and-a-half inches) "as a corrective, just in case
i start thinking a ton of cobblestones is worth as much as a few
diamonds." In all of Allen's work there was always evident the
literary sharpshooter's eye for the perfect word, phrase, figure of
speech, or rhythm. Yet when he declared his desire to be a writer, it
was with rueful self-deprecation.*

i can't bat out 40 pages of literature every week, but i can
usually turn out a good show . . . men like thurber, say, and
e.b. white, i can't hope to catch them now. they spent the last
30 years becoming fine artists. i spent them another way. ever
since the job in the library, i've had to think of money first.
well, it doesn't matter any more. i guess i'm doing what i want
to do. that's all i've ever done. through changes in the world—
a shrinkage of values—i've become successful. unless i get sick
i can go along this way for a long time. and eventually, i have
high hopes i'll be able to withdraw from the human race.

♦ ♦ ♦

we who attempt to write and amuse the masses, joust with futility.

♦ ♦ ♦

book—wish hunting in the subconscious.

♦ ♦ ♦

[as a writer] you have to be on your toes. some publisher may approach you to do the life of stonewall jackson and try to give you an advance in confederate money.

♦ ♦ ♦

a book is a small lamp hung out in the darkness of our time—to cheer us on the way.

♦ ♦ ♦

it's nice to be able to write. if you ever leave home in later life you can let the folks know where you are.

♦ ♦ ♦

each summer, i catch up with all of my reading and, when possible, endeavor to go through all of the worthwhile books i have collected over the winter period. if my eyes hold out i'll eventually become too intelligent to make a living in what is left of show business. the way things look in radio, and in the theatre, it will soon be necessary to undergo mental castration if one is to meet his public on level ground.

♦ ♦ ♦

Allen often mused about his writing in letters to authors he admired.

november
19th
1953

dear james thurber—

i want to thank you for sending me a copy of "thurber country."

you will not lose the royalty on my cuff volume. i had bought a copy before yours arrived. this will prove that i am not psychic.

if simon and schuster have done their job well i should be the only man in the world with two copies of "thurber country."

my lawyer will see you shortly about the inscription you have kindly added to my copy. you cannot be my greatest admirer since i am your greatest admirer. this is a form of adjective incest rarely practiced except by broadway columnists.

many years ago, harold ross wanted to try and make a writer of me. i told harold that when i saw that you were writing i planned to insert my quill back into the fowl.

who knows—if the foot had been on the other shoe—today you might be doing a lousy television program and i might be mailing you a copy of my new book "allen country."

sincerely—   F

♦ ♦ ♦

february 22, 1955

dear groucho—

since my book was published i have been busier than a good humor man on a hot day. i have been appearing on radio programs, tv shows, in bookshops, at séances and finally ended up with a super-book plug on a spectacular a medium was presenting on a ouija board.

whether these antics sell books i do not know. it seems to be the accepted practice in the book trade. the minute some deluded juggins writes a book he is supposed to be on the defensive. he is supposed to be at the beck and call of every dame who is hustling a book club to say a few words or he is to be available for a window appearance at sundry bookstores. mail is to be answered most of which comes from people who like to read but who do not buy books, hospitals who have small budgets but want the book for their libraries and church bazaars who want autographed copies to auction off to raise money to provide a low-hung deacon with a durable truss.

you touted me on to this writing thing. you are sitting snugly on your wafer-thin prat making a fortune and meeting a nice set of people on the program. i am fending off the dregs of the literati.

i went over to philadelphia recently. the sat eve post people want me to do an autobiography . . . i am considering the project. i've been talking to a number of old vaudeville actors but the research is too costly. i have been bitten during each interview. i got nothing and so far i have gone for a suit, a winter coat and too much money. mulling it over i don't think i could sustain an entire book on vaudeville. i might make use of some extraneous matter to embellish the chapters that would concern my experiences in the small-time domain.

if you are tired of it all and want to make a fortune without working i will let you in on my invention. it is sweeping church parishes around the country. i have patented a pulpit that can be turned into a bingo table. don't let hope and crosby grab this off. get in on it. i am also working on a long fly for short-armed men's trousers.

f. allen

◆ ◆ ◆

june 17th
1951

dear herman [*Wouk*]—

. . . success is something to cope with today. as soon as you have arrived at a point where attention is focused on you, it seems that hordes of maggoty little characters ooze out of your days to waste your time. today, there are so many pressure outfits and so many scurvy nobodies who somehow survive themselves through using other people for their negative purposes.

i have discussed this with john steinbeck on several occasions. it seems to me that a fellow who works hard to accomplish something has a problem to maintain the standard he has set for himself. after his initial success he should have time and the privacy he needs to enable him to continue to do good work. the writer's time is certainly worth more than the time of even a group of drones at some luncheon or some dynamic jerk who is attempting to use the writer to attract an audience for some fund-raising event.

the public has no time to waste on a failure. if you are a success you should have no time for the public since by comparison collectively the public is a failure. mark twain wrote "the skin of every human being contains a slave." also, "on security and a competence—that is the life that is best worth living." mark expressed my sentiments many years before i was able to make them known. i have always felt that the creative person derives most of his pleasure from his work. when he requires relaxation he can seek company.

i have the solution. if i could only write, i would be all set.

At the end of the 1930s, H. Allen Smith, a New York World-Telegram *reporter, interviewed Fred Allen, and they became friends. When Smith later wrote his first book,* Low Man on a Totem Pole, *he asked Allen (who would not crank up the courage or find time to attempt a book of his own for another fifteen years) to write the introduction.*

november 8th

1940

dear h. allen . . .

i finally found out what the h stands for. at least i thought i had found out. working in code i came to the conclusion that the h was for hernia. wednesday, however, i [was] advised . . . that you had been spared the hospital ordeal and that the two lumps were nothing but the after-effects of some bubblegum that had backfired, or something.

re the introduction. since you won't need it until next month, i can probably assemble some smithiana and turn it over to you. if it is suitable between us we should be able to fix up the grammar and if my name won't be a liability in merchandising the tome you are welcome to use it for any advertising purposes. when the book comes out, assuming that my preface is used (first assuming that it is written) i can even get a bit out of it on the program some week.

what with going on "information please" and turning up as the writer of a fragmentary contribution to a doubleday, doran publication i will soon be moving in the fadiman set, assuming that the fadiman set moves.

if you want to talk about the "who" treatise i can meet you next Tuesday at 3 P.M., in my atelier (which until recently i thought was one of two things that spurted from a deer's parietal area). if you are free we can discuss the "who" effort and the introduction. i will scare up some brilliant mots you can use. smith! the first man to put book-ends at each side of a psychopathic ward. smith! the first numismatist to collect his coins the hard way xraying gum slots to take to his studio. smith! the first writer to ever look to gravity to assure him that he will go down in history.

regards to mrs. smith and the sundry tiny smiths who roam your atelier. a word like that will bear repeating. sincerely . . .

f. allen (smith)

♦ ♦ ♦

november 21st
1940

dear h.a. . . .

have been thinking at odd moments about the introduction, or preface if you will, to your book. i say i have been thinking at odd moments. at even moments i have been attempting to get out the programs, truck with the mail, appease panhandlers and look from some gentleman on variety who said that i was verbose and made the information please broadcast dull entertainment. it isn't bad enough to waste an evening, appear gratis, but i have to get panned on top of it.

. . . soon . . . i will get started on my literary chore. will try to finish it semi-quickly. if it isn't right you will still have time to get a learned conspirator to lend a hand . . .

f. allen

♦ ♦ ♦

december
14th
1940

h.a.

am enclosing the enclosed.*

after noting its length i would suggest that you use what you have for the preface and make this the book.

---

*The introduction he wrote for Smith's book.

as you know this is not my racket.

the trouble i have is that there are so few minutes available that i cannot sit down at any one sitting and work out a mode of attack.

whatever is done has to be done in dribs and drabs. when a thing is done in a drib it is usually drab.

you can look this over.

you can do anything you want with it.

if you want to rewrite, cut, shrink, eliminate, etc. i, not being george bernard shaw, will have no objections.

if the idea is entirely off the beam you have my permission to throw the whole brochure away and approach gilbert seldes, or another craftsman who understands the business, to turn out something more suitable.

you can let me know what you think after you have waded through smith . . . in the aggregate.

. . . after i get wednesday's show on the air i shall have a little more time. if you feel that this matter can be used in one form, or another, i can meet you thursday, or friday, and discuss it . . .

f. allen

Fred Allen's introduction to Low Man on a Totem Pole.

The book you hold in your hand is the work of H. Allen Smith. It is published by Doubleday, Doran. Doubleday and Doran are enthusiastic about Mr. Smith's book. But if Doubleday and Doran *knew* Mr. Smith their enthusiasm would indeed be tested.

Mr. Smith is no harbinger of humdrum. Mr. Smith is no oracle of the orthodox. Mr. Smith hangs many strange portraits in his gallery of fantastic people. To Mr. Smith the world is a seething psychopathic ward, his fellow man just a pore-spattered husk that is concealing a story from Mr. Smith.

To Mr. Smith, the biographer who portrays the drab tycoon and the celebrity of the hour jousts with the trite. To Mr. Smith it is the little man, the neurotic nonentity, the tattered extrovert, the riff and raff whose lives are important. To those who slink through life fraught with insignificance he dedicates his pen. Mr. Smith is the screwballs' Boswell.

Who is this jetsam journalist H. Allen Smith? Longfellow wrote: "The smith, a mighty man is he." Longfellow gave no initials. The mighty smith couldn't have been H. Allen.

Nothing of Mr. Smith's was among the trivia buried in the Time Capsule at the World's Fair.

Ripley's records show that Smith has never gone over Niagara Falls in a beer firkin.

Smith has never thrown a forward pass that enabled Notre Dame to beat Army, or vice versa.

Who's Who lists several Smiths:

Smith, Adam, 1723–90. Scottish economist, lecturer on rhetoric and belles-lettres.

Smith, John, 1580–1631. American colonist. As Captain John this Smith gained some renown. An Indian girl, one Pocohantas, terminated a tribal peccadillo that involved Captain John from the neck up.

Smith, Brothers. Anticough crusaders. Popularized the snood-shaped beard and a licorice pellet to fend off coryza.

Smith, college for women, Northampton, Mass. H. Allen Smith has nothing to do with this.

Smith, Al, 1873–. American political leader. In 1936 gave practical demonstration of pedestrianism.

No, *Who's Who* makes no mention of H. Allen Smith. The Manhattan telephone directory lists four pages of Smiths. H. Allen is not among them. Who, then, is H. Allen Smith?

I have walked with H. Allen Smith. I know him like a book. It has been embarrassing knowing Smith like a book. I have caught myself several times making notes on his tongue so that I might refer back to some brilliant flight of fancy Smith has tossed off in casual conversation. As the man who knows Smith I have been asked to take him apart and see what makes him tick. If I get Smith apart my work is done. I shall make no effort to reassemble him. H. Allen Smith will be the first American author to go down to posterity in pieces.

He is a little man. He might be a midget who forgot himself and overgrew a few inches. Physically, Smith is a waste of skin. He weighs about one hundred and ten pounds with his bridge-work in and the complete works of Dale Carnegie under each arm. There isn't enough meat on him to glut a baby buzzard. At the cannibals' buffet Smith would be hors d'oeuvres. Jo Davidson could sculpt Smith in a pebble and have enough stone left over to gravel the bottom of a bird cage.

Organically, Smith is complete with heart, lungs, appendix and routine accessories. His legs have no calves and appear to be two swans' necks that have been starched. His arms dangle from their pits like two limp buggy whips from which his fingers sprout at the ends, looking like five scallion shoots.

Smith's face, which seems to be receding (from what, I am not prepared to say), hangs down from his hair and rests on his Adam's apple.

If Smith were an Indian he would be low man on any totem pole. His epidermis boasts no incision, birth mark, wart or tattoo display. As a mural Smith would be pretty dull. His complexion is a sort of sloppy pastel. When he flushes he turns the color of a meerschaum pipe that has been smoked twice. If Smith passed you in a Turkish bath (which is improbable) you wouldn't turn around. You would simply look at him and shrug your sheet.

Smith, sartorially, baffles description. He is at once the despair of the tailor and the moth. His overcoat appears to be a tight Inverness with mess-jacket sleeves. His hat is felt at a disadvantage. Even the tiny feather that juts from his hatband seems to be moulting. His suit is a rhapsody in rummage. The coat cascades from his clavicle and sort of peters out north of his sacral plexus. The horizontal wrinkles of the cloth give one the impression that Smith is standing behind a tweed Venetian blind. His vest hangs down like a cloth noose. At first glance it appears to be a sarong with no sense of direction. His Elk's tooth has a cavity in it. His trousers bag from the hips down. From the front they look like herringbone funnels. In profile you find they are butt sprung and sag in the back like cloth jowls. Smith's haberdashery is the talk of surrealist circles. His necktie is a cross between a hawser that comes with a toy boat and three feet of twine in technicolor. His shoes can only be described as leather figments of a demented cobbler's imagination. In general appearance Smith can only be saluted as Saroyan's conception of a white-collar worker.

From tender infancy Smith has been an early riser. He sleeps so little that Orpheus barely knows him by sight. When he dreams he only has time for a synopsis. He was the first man to discover that you can cut a sleeping pill in half and enjoy a nap.

He eats as sparingly as he sleeps. A calorie, or two, constitutes a hearty breakfast. Einstein reduced vitamin B-1 to B-½ to accommodate Smith. As a result of his infrequent eating Smith's teeth have become hypersensitive. He seldom uses a toothpick unless it has been warmed to the temperature of his gums.

As he stands today, Smith doesn't imbibe. He has nothing against alcohol, save that it arouses in his breast an urge to fly kites in two-room apartments. He smokes incessantly and is forever borrowing cigarettes and matches. Whenever he finds himself destitute of matches he creates fire by rubbing two Boy Scouts together.

His hobbies have been many and variegated. Until his eyes went bad his hobby was reading the literature printed on small breakfast-food boxes. With the exception of two bran barons and a nearsighted housewife in Jersey City, Smith at one time was the only man living who knew the vital information those flake sarcophagi held.

His current hobby is reading quickly. If a story in *Liberty* specifies: "Reading time, 12 minutes," Smith will read it in five and save seven minutes. Last year the minutes saved reading *Liberty* stories under par added up to six days and enabled Smith to enjoy almost an extra week on his vacation (which he spent practicing). In a recent speed-reading exhibition Smith sat in a dark room, and a news photographer set off a flashlight bulb. During the ensuing split second of glare Smith read an entire "My Day" column and got halfway through Pegler.

He has many other part-time hobbies. He enjoys looking at people who are looking at excavations. He stands in long lines outside of movie theatres and, at the crucial moment, doesn't go in. Displayed prominently in his study is an old-fashioned chamber pot (with handle) which bears the sign: "I'm going to get this full of money."

As for his work: By profession H. Allen Smith is a news-paperman. By choice he is a biographer to the dispensable man. His routine work on the paper is essentially a side line. On his way to cover an assignment Smith's beady eyes will fluoroscope his immediate vicinity. His nose samples each breeze for a chance scent of interview fodder. Doorways are scanned, alleys are rummaged, manhole covers are tilted—just in case.

Smith never knows where his next screwball is coming from. His world is his laboratory, the human race his clinic, the nearest disciple of monomania's story his immediate concern. He will walk twenty miles to hear a cliché—and frequently does. If there is one man in the world who knows how the other half lives (which half escapes me at the moment) and writes about it that man is H. Allen Smith.

Any similarity between the Smith taken apart in the preceding paragraphs and the author of this book is purely incidental. If this cameo were to appear in a digest magazine brevity and honesty would reduce an assay of Mr. Smith to these simple facts:

He deals in legends of strange men and women.

He is gainfully employed on the staff of the *New York World-Telegram.*

He is a feature writer of renown.

He is known as one of the best rewrite men rampant in the newspaper world today.

He is happily married and the father of two children.

He is a good man.

His first name is Harry.

He has written a book I am sure you will enjoy. If you want to curl up with a good book start curling up and turn this page.

Fred Allen

Low Man on a Totem Pole *and his subsequent books (*Life in a Putty Knife Factory, *etc.) made Smith for many years the best-selling humor author in America.*

april 1st
1941

dear low . . .

scrivened fun has a far better chance than oral fun. that, to me, is radio's greatest problem for our type of show. instead of pointing everything for a certain class of listener at home all of the humor has to be lowered and played in a bass clef motif to get an audible reaction from the majority of the yuks who make a racket of broadcast-going. with scrivened fun . . . there it is . . . you can read it, weigh it, work it out and finally enjoy it. oral fun is heard once by the hearee and its reaction can be marred by a thousand and one things rampant as the oral jibes are being dispensed . . .

"omar—the preface writer"

♦ ♦ ♦

may third
1941

loch . . .

this is the scot preamble to "low man" . . . used here as a salutation. i told you the damn book would cause a hernia to sprout in the peaceful loins of your ideal existence. come fame . . . you are a marked man. no longer will you be able to stand back and adjust your myopia to scan the clod and the exponent of the non compos mentis. you will be under scrutiny from now on. lou sobol will chronicle your every move, ed sullivan will invite you to appear on his summer radio program . . . for free . . . your name will be added to all the sucker and chump lists. real estate men will try to sell you an estate. house and garden will want a subscription. that sonofabitz who operates "who's who" will make your life a hot-foot. better to be named in "who's thro" and know that you can prowl around a nonentity than to be lionized and known from coast to coast "low man on the scrotum pole." christ, smith! you've done it!

"preface peter"

♦ ♦ ♦

Allen wrote the following essay after completing his first book, Treadmill to Oblivion.

The New Author

the minute an author has a book published he is in demand. his relatives and friends clamor around him eager to obtain free copies. strangers are suddenly inviting him to cocktail parties to meet other strangers. little old ladies are dragging him off to address their dog watching clubs. bartenders start asking him for his autograph and begin to save old olives he leaves in his martini glass as souvenirs. radio and television personalities implore the author to appear on their programs to discuss his book and to expound his views on politics and put the world's affairs in order.

this is not idle conjecture, irate reader. (i have never seen a gentle reader.) these thing(s) have been happening to me. i recently had a book "treadmill to oblivion" published. before my book appeared, when my relatives and friends and i met at the unemployment insurance office, they avoided me. when i showed up at a cocktail party, all conversation stopped abruptly and the host would hide the gin. little old ladies trembled when i passed by and buried their heads in their shawls. bartenders turned off their hearing aids and walked down to the other end of the bar when i ordered. radio and tv personalities weren't interested in my opinions or in me.

since "treadmill to oblivion" has made its appearance on the book counters around the country, i have been busier than a chinaman trying to eat with one chopstick. my days are fraught with appointments. (i have been asked to address the audubon society on "molting." discuss a new doughnut recipe with the salvation army chief. speak with a group of plumbers who would rather be einsteins.) my nights are crammed with social glitter and literate fripperies. (appearing in motion picture theatre lobbies for the opening of a new popcorn machine. throwing out the first ping pong ball at the table tennis tournament. taking a bow on all fours at the horse show.) my mail is redundant with requests to comment on minor phases of my life or to divulge my reactions to forces that have tinkered with my ambitions.

a recent question arrived from the chicago tribune book editor. the question is "what books have influenced you during your life?" my answer is "many books have influenced me."

as a baby a book, an old webster's dictionary, played an important part in my pablum period. the cane bottom on my highchair was broken. when i sat down to eat i would slip through the hole. my tiny arms were not long enough to enable me to reach my food. when I sat on the webster's dictionary, however, my baby viands were accessible. the first book to influence my life sustained it. i was able to reach sufficient food to survive.

at grammar school, a book (pilgrim's progress) helped me to acquire an education. as a small boy i attended a rural school. our teacher was a frail creature named miss travis. in one corner of the classroom there was a mousehole. every morning, as class started, an inquisitive mouse looked through the rodent aperture. when miss travis saw the mouse she would start to scream. i would throw pilgrim's progress at the mouse. the mouse would withdraw and miss travis would return to her teaching. without pilgrim's progress' influence i would have graduated from school nothing but an authority on screams.

while coping with adolescence, I worked in the boston public library. many books influenced me there. carrying bundles of books developed my arms. delivering the books to readers made my legs strong and sturdy. without these books i might have grown up a weakling.

after i was married, one book influenced me greatly. it was the *fanny farmer cook book.* through this book portland mastered the art of cooking and preparing food. if i had been forced to eat raw meat i might have turned to cannibalism. without the influence of the *fanny farmer cook book,* today, when i say "i'm having a friend for dinner," i would mean it.

when i started to become a comedian many books influenced me. the books of men who had fomented fun down through the years: humorists artemas ward, bill nye, josh billings, eugene field, mark twain, finley peter dunne, stephen leacock, robert benchley, ring lardner, james thurber, sid perelman and many others.

now that i have become an author (*treadmill to oblivion*) i am like all living authors today. there is one book about which we are concerned. it is the only book that influences an author. it is his bank book.

Allen was, of course, an omnivorous reader and bibliophile. His personal library of approximately 900 volumes ran the gamut from humor to classic fiction, plus books on folklore, poetry, medicine, movies, cartoons, language, writing, drama, politics, boxing, criticism, psychology, history, criminal investigation and philosophy.

♦ ♦ ♦

(On publishers)
they have all bewildered me. most of them survive through manipulating the works of others while they themselves concentrate on drinking or social contacts. as a class they are too precious for me. i am always afraid that i will lean against a publisher and chip or break him.

♦ ♦ ♦

(On writers)

on several occasions i have argued with john steinbeck. i claim that when a writer becomes successful, generally without giving it too much thought, he assumes another style of living. with the introduction of luxury into his life he withdraws from his old friends, haunts and the contacts that have enabled him to find material that made him successful in the first place. john says it isn't true but i don't think you can come out of the stork club with your belly full and caviar rolling down your vest and rush home and write a "grapes of wrath." john says you can. so i must be wrong.

only piece for *the new yorker*

In the 1930s, shortly after the birth of The New Yorker, *Allen was a sensation on Broadway as performer and writer of comedy sketches in a succession of revues.*

Harold Ross and his managing editor, Woolcott Gibbs, fans of the comedian, encouraged him to submit something to the new publication. The piece appeared in the January 10, 1931, issue (an ad for Washington's elegant Shoreham Hotel on the page beside Allen's piece offers a single room for $5.00, a double at $8.00). This was about two years before Allen, then thirty-seven, broke into radio. Though "Don't Trust Midgets" may seem a bit labored to our ears seven decades after it was written, it appears here as an early example of Allen's evolving comic sensibility in the context of the emerging sophisticated urban humor typified by the fledgling magazine. The article is estimable, if only for the phrase "German bon mots."

Allen was turned down on the next piece he submitted. He never submitted another.

Don't Trust Midgets

The reason you have to stand in the lobbies of moving-picture theatres waiting to see the show, and the reason you can seldom get a seat once you are inside the theatre, is because certain people who have no home ties and no personal belongings are living in movie cathedrals. Another type of person, minus a sense of humor, lives in the vaudeville theatres where the seats are not reserved. In order to eliminate standing in the lobbies of all theatres where the shows are continuous, the following True Confession is offered to the theatre going public, in hopes that it will remedy this evil:

I, Sylvester Prebble, apple-vendor (and, incidentally, the first apple-salesman to ignore the corner location and open my crate in the middle of the block), hereby attest the following to be true facts of my case. I trusted a midget and have slowly receded from a habitual theatre goer to an orchard middleman. This is my story, so help me God.

(Signed) SYLVESTER PREBBLE

Ten years ago I was devoted to the theatre and spent every night after work (I was an eggnog inspector at Leggett's but due to the fact that people ceased to be eggnog-conscious around 1920, my duties were light) at some vaudeville or movie theatre. This went on for two years and my love for the theatre became so great that I would rush out between eggnog inspections and see a show during the afternoon.

Completely gripped by a mania for entertainment, it wasn't long before I was spending twenty of the twenty-four hours of the day rushing from show to show. "This can't go on," I said to myself; but being hard of hearing, I must have talked too loud, for the manager of the drugstore overheard me and replied: "You're damn right, Prebble. This can't go on. You're fired. We can thank your laxity for the figures which prove that our eggnog business has fallen off two hundred percent in the last eighteen months. If you're so fond of the theatre, why don't you live in it?"

Here was an idea. Now that I was out of work, I would have more time on my hands—although not a great deal more. Living in a theatre would be ideal. Nursing this thought,

I rushed to my room, packed all my clothes, making sure to take heavy underwear for the summer months when the cooling system would be working, gathered my percolator, provisions, and a gunny sack full of personal belongings, and bought a ticket to the Gargantua Theatre.

The shows at the Gargantua changed twice weekly, which relieved the monotony. I spent a very pleasant year in the Z row of the orchestra. The second year I moved to the centre of the theatre. My deafness, which had caused me to lose my position as eggnog overseer, again asserted itself and in order to hear the vaudeville distinctly, I thought it better to move nearer the stage.

I was very happy in K row for over three years when my hearing became so bad that I had to move to the first row, where I cooked, read, slept, and otherwise enjoyed myself for another year. The shows were fine, the ushers cordial; I think this was really the happiest year of my life at the Gargantua.

Dame Fortune deserted me, however. I could scarcely hear anything spoken on the stage and, rather than leave the theatre I had learned to love, I spent the following year in the orchestra pit, posing as a cymbal-player. None of the vaudeville acts ever had parts for cymbal-players, so I spent some thirteen months enjoying the shows, laughing in the right places, applauding enthusiastically, while sitting next to the drummer.

Again my luck gave out. The next spring my deafness became so bad that the only way I could hear a word of what was going on was to go up onto the stage and stand next to the actor who was speaking. This I did for several months, with great success. No one ever molested me. The audience thought that I was a master of ceremonies and, since I never said anything, the actors thought I was the manager of the theatre. Things ran smoothly.

I say that things ran smoothly until the week that Finger's Midgets played the Gargantua. I noticed that when I walked around the stage during their act, trying to hear the German bon mots, the audience laughed more at me than at the actual performers. Mr. Finger, as soon as he discovered that I was not the house manager, offered me a position in his act. The act was to remain the same except that I would come out and listen to the dialogue and follow the actors around.

One little midget, Stephen by name, leaned over to me and said: "Stick to Mr. Finger and you will be a big man." Foolishly, I listened to that cursed midget. I sold my equipment, stove and all, and joined Finger's Midgets. After two years, more or less uneventful, without salary—I had forgotten to speak to Mr. Finger about this matter before leaving the theatre—I decided to assert myself. Buttonholing Finger about this matter after a matinee, I said: "See here, Finger, what about my salary?"

"Salary?" he thundered. "I like your nerve. Who do you think you are?" he demanded, turning on me with the fury of a wildcat cornered.

"I know who I am," I answered coolly, not wishing to make a scene. "I'm the man who spent nearly eight years in the Gargantua Theatre and gave up my future there to come with your act. That's who I am."

"That has nothing to do with the matter of salary," echoed Finger. "What makes you think that you should be paid?"

He nearly had me, but I feinted mentally. "Don't put on the dog, Finger," I challenged as he reached for his raccoon coat. "Stephen, your prize dwarf, told me in so many words: 'Stick with Mr. Finger and you will be a big man.' I've been with your midgets for two years." Tears welled to my eyes, as I continued. "Look at me. Working with midgets for two years. Am I a big man?"

"Only by comparison," concluded Finger, throwing a midget at me as he stalked through the door.

That is why I say: "Never trust a midget," or you, too, will be selling apples, as I find myself doing today. It took me ten years to WAKE UP, otherwise I would have been out of the Gargantua Theatre after the first show, and someone would have had a seat instead of standing in the lobby for all those years. If it didn't take people so long to wake up, there would always be seats available at your favorite movie theatre and the lobby, as we know it today, with its milling throngs, would be a thing of the past, even as eggnog inspecting.

—Fred Allen

a yearning

Once—asked by a Time *interviewer "What is your supreme ambition?"—Fred Allen said, "Write, if I had the brains."*

He did. And he did.

glossary

Following is a list of people, places and things mentioned in the text, which relate to Allen's time.

Abbot—title of elected first officer of the Friars Club, same as president.

Adrian—early Hollywood costume designer.

AFTRA—American Federation of Television and Radio Artists, the union.

Air Warden—volunteers during WWII who patrolled neighborhoods to keep lights off.

Aquacade—*see* Rose, Billy.

Atwell, Roy—a regular on Allen's show, whose specialty was battering language.

Baker, Phil—a successful radio comedian of the 1930s.

Beaver in every pot—a take-off of Depression-era political campaign promises (e.g., "A chicken in every pot.")

Benny Goodman picture—*The Benny Goodman Story,* the 1956 movie, starring Steve Allen as Goodman.

Blue Eagle—the graphic symbol of the N.R.A. (National Recovery Act), a government program during the Depression.

Byrnes, James—FDR friend and chief of staff.

Cantor, Eddie—stage, film and radio comedian with banjo eyes and five daughters.

Capp, Al—creator of "Li'l Abner" comic strip.

Carnera, Primo—took the heavyweight title from Jack Sharkey in 1933.

Davidson, Jo—renowned American sculptor, 1883–1952.

Dillinger, John—"Public Enemy number 1," killed by FBI in 1934.

Dionne Quintuplets—five girls born in Ontario in 1934.

Double or Nothing—1940s quiz show.

Dowling, Eddie—song-and-dance man and theatre producer.

Downbeat—a music trade magazine, the *Rolling Stone* of the 1940s.

Edwards, Ralph—host of radio and TV show *This Is Your Life*, which celebrated the famous by bringing them face-to-face with people from their pasts.

Fadiman, Clifton—writer, book editor and host of *Information Please.*

Fireside Chats of FDR—regular radio addresses of President Franklin D. Roosevelt.

Gangbusters—dramatic crime anthology of the 1930s and 1940s.

Gas Coupons—during WWII, gasoline was rationed to civilian car owners.

Godfrey, Arthur—briefly Allen's announcer in the 1940s, who became for a time the most listened-to person in America on radio and television.

Greenstreet, Sidney—the fat man in the white suit in *Casablanca.*

Hadacol—potent alcohol-saturated, vitamin-mineral elixir hawked on the Hank Williams radio show of the late 1940s.

Harry (little old Harry)—in Senator Claghorn sketch (page 142) refers to President Harry Truman.

Hines, Duncan—1930s and 1940s restaurant critic, early version of what the Zagat Survey is today.

Hooper Rating—radio rating to measure the number of program listeners.

Hoover, Herbert—thirty-first president, called Herby by Senator Claghorn.

Information Please—the most literate, longest-running radio show of its day (1938–1952), hosted by Clifton Fadiman. The regular panel was made up of John Kieran, Oscar Levant, and Franklin P. Adams, plus a weekly guest—sometimes Fred Allen.

Jessel, George—vaudeville contemporary of Allen who later gained fame as a movie producer and glib toastmaster.

Jolson, Al—singer–blackface performer who starred in *The Jazz Singer,* the first talking picture.

Jones, Spike—his City Slickers orchestra performed parodies of well-known songs.

Kibbee, Guy—bald, baby-faced movie character actor.

Kreisler, Fritz—early twentieth-century violin virtuoso.

LaGuardia, Fiorello H.—New York City mayor (1934–1945); nicknamed the "Little Flower."

Legett's—popular Manhattan drugstore meeting place.

Liberty—magazine of general interest that prefaced each article with the phrase "Reading Time," followed by the estimated number of minutes it would require to complete the piece.

Lindy's—renowned Broadway restaurant show-biz hangout, now defunct.

Lombardo, Guy—celebrity orchestra leader.

Lox—Mrs. Nussbaum's mispronunciation of Lux, then popular soap flakes.

Ma Perkins—a daily radio serial about Ma Perkins, an affable, wise widow whose decency and humanity endeared her to listeners for twenty-seven years (1933–1960).

Manhattan Merry-Go Round—an alternate to *Your Hit Parade*, which featured performances of the eight top songs in sheet-music sales. The show's life exactly matched Allen's—1932 to 1949.

Marquis, Don—newspaper columnist, creator of Archie, the cockroach, who, after the newspaper closed at night, dove headlong onto the typewriter keys to write poetic columns. Like Allen, Archie typed in lowercase only.

Marshall Plan—1947 program of George Marshall, secretary of state, to rehabilitate war-torn Europe with U.S. aid.

Martin, Freddy—bandleader famous for adapting Tchaikovsky's First Piano Concerto in B-flat into the hit 1941 ballad "Tonight We Love."

McBride, Mary Margaret—popular daily radio interviewer.

Minsky's—legendary burlesque theatre founded in the nineteenth century.

Montfort's, Mrs.—the Manhattan theatrical boardinghouse Allen stayed in as a young vaudeville performer, written about extensively in *Much Ado About Me*.

Morgan, Henry—acerbic radio comedian mentored by Allen.

Morgenthau, Henry, Jr.—FDR's secretary of the treasury.

Mussolini, Benito—fascist premier of Italy during WWII.

"My Day"—syndicated newspaper column written by Eleanor Roosevelt.

N.V.A.—National Vaudeville Association.

Olsen and Johnson—comic duo stars of *Hellzapoppin,* a hit Broadway revue of the 1940s.

Pathé News—the theatrical newsreel Allen parodied in his 1920s *Variety* column as *Passé News* (see page xxvi), likely the breeding ground for his *Town Hall Tonight* news items that have influenced legions of comedy shows since.

Pegler, Westbrook—powerful, vengeful, conservative political columnist of Allen's time.

Penner, Joe—radio comic, whose silly catchphrases "Wanna buy a duck?" "You naaaasty maaaan!" and "You vicious viper!" were briefly popular in the early 1930s.

Rockwell, Doc—Allen's vaudeville colleague and longtime Maine friend, who traditionally appeared on Allen's final show of the season.

Rose, Billy—colorful stage producer and theatre owner who produced such theatrical extravaganzas as the Aquacade, a 1940 San Francisco World's Fair attraction that launched the film career of Esther Williams.

Rumpelmayers—legendary ice cream and hot chocolate parlor in Manhattan's St. Moritz Hotel, now, alas, gone.

Sabu—young East Indian star of a series of movies in which he rode an elephant.

Saroyan, William—Pulitizer Prize–winning playwright and author.

Sharkey, Jack—*see* Carnera, Primo.

Sheen, Bishop Fulton J.—popular TV and radio priest in early years of television.

Smith, Kate—portly singer on popular weekly radio show— famous for singing "God Bless America."

Sobol, Lou—New York gossip columnist.

Texas Company—manufacturers of Texaco gasoline, one of Allen's radio sponsors in the 1940s.

Victory Garden—to forestall food shortages during WWII, citizens were encouraged to grow their own vegetables.

Wagner Act—officially, the National Labor Relations Act (of 1935). Law to guarantee the rights of workers to form a union and engage in collective bargaining, named for Senator Robert F. Wagner, Demorcrat, N.Y.

What Makes Sammy Run?—1940s novel by Budd Schulberg.

Wons, Tony—his intimate, sappy, greeting card-style chats were popular with women radio listeners in the 1930s.